Spiritual Power

Transcripts from several discourses given by

Mark Griffin

The Summer Retreat ~ June, 2008
Weekly Meeting ~ July 3, 2008
Weekly Meeting ~ July 10, 2008
Weekly Meeting ~ August 7, 2008
Intensive ~ July 19, 2008

Hard Light Center of Awakening

Spiritual Power © 2008 by Mark Griffin,
Hard Light Center of Awakening
ISBN 978-0-975902-09-7

All rights reserved. No part of this book may be reproduced in any form or by any means, electronic or mechanical, including photocopying, recording, or by any information storage and retrieval system, without the express written permission from the author.

For more information about the **Hard Light Center of Awakening** please visit *www.hardlight.org*. The web site provides a complete listing of Mark Griffin's other books and CDs, as well as links to audiobooks, podcasts and PDF books.

The **Hard Light Center of Awakening** is an organization founded and directed by Mark Griffin as a forum for the study of spirituality and meditation. Mark Griffin is a Meditation Master who is firmly established in the advanced Nirvikalpa Samadhi states — rare strands of consciousness that lead to remarkable perception and spiritual accomplishment.

First Edition: December 31, 2008

Transcription: Ann Brockway and Cynthia Stevenson
Additional thanks to Pamela Grant

Editing, Layout: PodPublishing

TABLE OF CONTENTS

The Siddha Lineage viii

Introduction. x

The 2008 Joshua Tree Summer Retreat

    Orientation 1

    Day One. 8

    Day Two 41

    Day Three 59

Weekly Meeting #1. 114

Weekly Meeting #2. 128

Weekly Meeting #3. 151

All-Day Intensive 162

Glossary. 188

Further Resources. 209

The Siddha Lineage

Mark Griffin is a Westerner who was born in the 1950's in the Pacific Northwest. His early adult years were spent in the aggressive pursuit of higher knowledge and purpose.

While a young man, Mark's studies in art and music brought him to the San Francisco Bay area. There in 1976 he met his Guru, Baba Muktananda. After years of full-time immersion in the study of meditation, Mark encountered a milestone of extreme spiritual significance – entrance into the advanced state of consciousness known as Nirvikalpa Samadhi. After Muktananda died, Mark continued to study with the great teachers of the Kagyu tradition, Kalu Rinpoche and Chogyam Trungpa, who supported the maturing and stabilizing of his abilities.

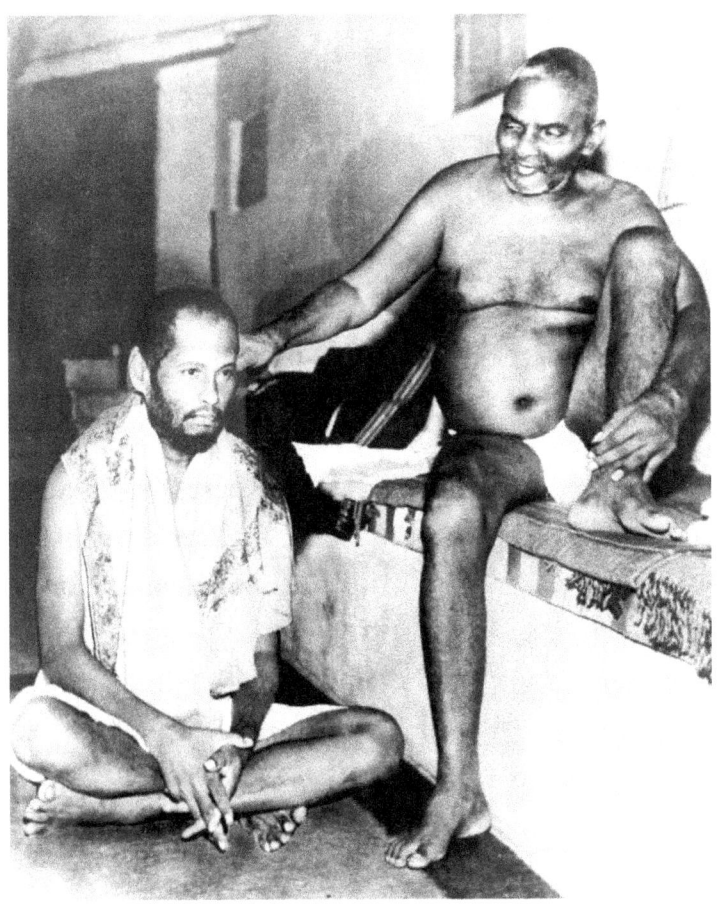

In 1989, after attracting several interested students, Mark began to teach meditation. He and his students relocated to Los Angeles and started the Hard Light Center of Awakening, an association dedicated to the art and science of awareness of the Self.

When Mark Griffin met Baba Muktananda he immediately realized that Baba was his Guru, his true teacher. Baba's Guru was the great saint of India, Bhagawan Nityananda of Ganeshpuri. It is with the blessings of these remarkable Siddhas that Mark carries on his inspiring teachings.

– INTRODUCTION –

In the summer of 2008, Mark Griffin led the members of the Hard Light Center of Awakening on an amazing journey into the experience and study of Spiritual Power.

It began with a three and a half day silent retreat near Joshua Tree National Park, in the desert of Southern California. Joshua Tree is home to several significant power vortices, so it was a perfect environment for this immersion. The impact of the retreat was so profound on all those who participated that Mark felt it important to continue the study in the next three regular weekly meetings, and on into the following Intensive.

This book contains the entirety of that retreat, as well as the four following sessions. You'll find that many more topics are addressed by Mark in these talks, beyond strictly talking about spiritual power per se - yet all of the topics discussed are viewed through this particular lens – What is spiritual power, and what does it mean for a spiritual seeker to have access to raw spiritual power?

PodPublishing, Editors

"One of the benefits of this retreat will be a huge deposit of power into the stream of your mind, body, being. This is the kind of setting where movement between the planes is very, very easy. A simple tap on the doorway will draw enormous energy into your system – energy that is quite endless. I guess what I'm trying to say is that meditating on power is fun, and like anything that is truly fun, it is also a little dangerous."

Mark Duffy

JOSHUA TREE SUMMER SOLSTICE RETREAT

Orientation

Welcome to the retreat. During these next seventy-two hours, we will be using all of the human form – body, speech and mind – to align and merge with the focus of our retreat: the power and light of God.

Our session this evening is a point of assembly. We've all spent the day traveling to this place, and now we stand at the doorway to the retreat. First and foremost, the retreat is an opportunity to turn within. The idea behind the retreat is to withdraw to a place of peace and isolation. For the term of the retreat, we will withdraw our consciousness from the surface appearance of the world and turn inward. The retreat is designed so that you can move through the structure of the day without having to externalize at all. The entire tempo and schedule is set to basically move like clockwork. It's kind of like getting on to a moving river and moving with the flow of that current. The basic format of the retreat will be meditation, both formal and deep sitting meditation, as well as walking meditation.

There's a very powerful psychological doorway between sitting still and turning within, and standing up and moving about. On retreat, you have an opportunity to study how your attention moves on both sides of that fulcrum, to find the point of internalization and externalization of attention, and practice the skill to be able to deeply internalize and externalize at will.

When you sit quietly, it is very easy and natural to turn within, but when you stand up and begin to move about the world, you spontaneously externalize, and there's a very powerful shift of attention. With just a little bit of training and attention to the matter, you can learn to split your attention between the internal and external while you are in standing-and-moving-about mode. Over the course of the twelve hours of meditation we have each day on retreat, you'll be practicing both the sitting and walking meditation modes.

One of the advantages of spiritual training here in Joshua Tree is hidden in the nature of the desert itself – it is the reflex of power. Power is one of the natural qualities of the desert, so you'll find in the nature of the meditations we have here, a very strong movement of the power of God, expressed in the kundalini. When you are in a place that is empty, attention moves very swiftly, very forcefully. The movement between planes has a very dynamic and vibrant tone to it. It is swiftly moving and dramatic. We'll be taking advantage of this over the course of the retreat.

One of the other benefits of the desert retreat is that, because it is a place where there are very few human beings, the structure of the external and visible world and the structure of the internal and invisible world are almost equally apparent. So the interaction between the planes is also one of the qualities of meditation in the desert. I think you'll find it very interesting. The desert has a drama to it. I went through a phase of doing retreats here in this facility a few years ago, and I'm familiar with the architecture of this area.

Whenever the use of the word power is involved, you're dealing with the kundalini, the electrical force that is behind the throb of creation, the electrical force of the prana shakti, or the life force. It is that power that moves with great speed and intensity in the desert. So it's important that you stay very aligned with your yogic principles and spiritual training. Stay grounded, stay aligned with the breath, stay aware of the presence of gravity, and become aware of how the assembly point of awareness moves between the four bodies of matter, energy, mind, and essence – the Atman, or supra-conscious.

I've deliberately introduced the retreat as a relationship between the alignment of the structure of the human form and the light and power of God. It is form and consciousness. We will be using both the superpowers of consciousness and the kundalini throughout the retreat. We will use the SoHam to stay centered and aligned with the breath. Again, because the desert is a place where very few people are, it is more attuned to the force of nature.

In the yoga tantra, everything comes through the medicine wheel. Many clues are given about how the wheel will operate by looking and listening to the speech of the earth. On the stage of the desert we also have the drama of the heat. I want everyone to be conscious of your interaction with the heat. We will be doing short walks throughout the day. Everyone should stay hydrated.

This retreat, as I said, offers an opportunity to study the alignment of body, speech and mind, with the light and power of God. It's going to be an opportunity for you to experience the intense movement of spiritual energy, experiment with your relationship to it, and come to find a way to be with that profound presence and that profound force. Basic principles of spiritual training and the yoga tantra such as the deep cycling of the bellows breathing, the alignment with the SoHam and pressing the consciousness into the space between the breaths will keep you centered and grounded.

As the consciousness moves, you'll find that the poles between the crown of the head and the base of the spine become very dramatically impacted by the movement of light. This will be the place where the retreat actually occurs. You will feel the presence of spirit directly applied to your system, with a deep and swiftly moving tempo. The focus of the retreat will be one of internal and external speech, happening simultaneously.

It's very important that once you enter retreat, you participate completely in the flow of retreat. It is very much like getting on a canoe and setting downstream. As we move downstream, it picks up speed. Because we're dealing directly with light and power, there will be lots of very interesting and dramatic shifts in the water.

Meditation in the desert is very amazing. The division between the planes can be very transparent, and the opportunity is very available in this kind of setting to see the true face of the world. As you awaken, you step into a much more sophisticated universe than you first thought; the quality and sheer number of sentient beings are vastly greater.

Once the retreat formally starts tomorrow, we will be engaging in the rule of silence. Everyone will maintain silence and maintain internalization throughout the course of the retreat. This is simply to keep the mind turned inward. After you spend even a few hours in meditation, you become very aware of how much it takes to externalize your consciousness, to speak and to listen to others. By generating the intention of silence, your attention will naturally be pressed inward.

The retreat is the opportunity to plunge within. We pick the time and place, and then generate concentrated spiritual force so that we may pass through the doorway into reality. The idea of retreat is a profound and simple one: sitting with yourself, removing the barriers and shadows between your awareness and your true nature. You come to the retreat with the intention to address your consciousness with focus and intensity on the truth that is present within you, as you. It's very simple and very powerful. It is an opportunity.

Spiritual life is not a life of theory, it is a life of experience. As anybody who has cared to look knows, life takes place both in light and shadow. The desert has a way of clearing the way and generating insight. You learn something about yourself. The impact of spiritual power is like a strong wind. It is important to embrace the spirit of Bodhicitta – it keeps the mind and the heart balanced, and it keeps the body comfortable. Use your understanding of the human form – the system of the three rivers, ida pingala and sushumna, how the six seats of the chakras operate and the breath and the space between the breaths. To be involved in the dynamics of power and light requires relaxation, relaxation, relaxation. Hang loose. The nature of the medicine wheel and the nature of the desert bring a unique and special drama to the retreat.

Very good. We'll meet in the morning and begin.

Good night.

SUMMER SOLSTICE RETREAT
DAY ONE

Good morning, everyone. I would like to welcome you all with love to the Summer Solstice 2008 retreat, here at Mental Physics, Joshua Tree.

Let's start the ball rolling by taking thirty minutes of silence and meditation to establish our seat, putting our best foot forward for the next three days. I always find the beginning of retreats very interesting. There's something about them that's very simple, direct and very Zen, knowing and feeling within our hearts that we are dedicating these next seventy-two hours to consciousness. We establish a quiet, deep feeling of intention to stay connected to the stream, like standing on the edge of a pool just before you start a 10,000 meter swim.

Everyone begin the cycling of the deep bellows breath. Relax and align the body with gravity. In long meditations, gravity is your friend. Listen to the vibration, the throb of the SoHam, the prana/apana, the rising and falling of the breath. Press into the space between the breaths. Here in the beginning, the relationship is crystal clear. Feel the space of your own mind and body, speech, and mind, and the layers of the four bodies. Reach deeply within yourself. You should also become aware that you're surrounded by a presence, a pressure, a vibration. This is the mandala of the retreat you are about to enter. This medicine wheel has a very distinct feeling. You can sense immediately the presence of the desert. This area is very powerful and is somewhat complex. Become aware of the light and power of God. We will begin. (meditation)

In the old days, we used to say that God lived in the desert. This place is interesting because it's right on the ragged edge.

Once again, I would like to welcome everyone to the Summer Solstice Retreat. Today is the day of the summer solstice, arising in the late afternoon at 4:59. The change in seasons is when the particles of space and time change their mode of operation. They behave differently, activated by light and dark, coolness and heat, and by the change in the operation of gravity. This is the perfect place for our summer solstice this year, as it is a very respectable power vortex.

We have certainly sat in vortices together before in our Hard Light retreats – in Varanasi, the Cosmic Cave, Nimboli, Ganeshpuri, Meher Mount, Meherabad and Taos. But there is an interesting note of difference in that all of those places have rulers, or have a dominant energy. In most cases, they are dominated by the forces of dharma, and have a lot of track laid inside them. They have been used for generating spiritual and dharma work, both personal and universal, for many centuries, even kalpas.

The vortex here in Joshua Tree is a very strong vortex that has no rulers, other than the usual set of ruffians that take up their homes here. It's a kind of "anything goes" place. It is equally dark and light, and operates equally in light and shadow. It makes it very interesting, and it activates both the left and right side of the brain. Because it is of the nature of power and because it has no rulers, it is without conscience. It simply exists, as itself.

Right now, and for the next few days, I am the ruler. I come in with my gang, backed up by the lineage. It's easy. I decided to do this intensive in this way, because I wanted you to have an opportunity to experience, experiment and play with power, to swim in the unseen space of consciousness, to swim in the waters of power.

Water is a metaphor in the yoga tantra for meditation. Speaking of water, the ocean and swimming is a good projection of meditation and spiritual training, because when you deal with the yoga tantra, quite simply, you can't swim without getting wet. You have to plunge in and deal with the dynamics of the water. Anybody that has swum in the ocean knows that it can be anything, and you have to respond to a thousand different factors every ten seconds. You have to rely on your own strength, your coordination, your will, and your awareness. You pay attention to what's going on. If you do that, everything is great and you have a wonderful afternoon. But at any moment, a surprise can arise and move the situation out of your control. You have to respond with clarity, intensity and inspiration, or you'll get hurt.

This is exactly what it's like in spiritual training, and especially in dealing with power. It is one of the true tests of a person's nature. You always truly see what a person is about when they begin to have contact with power, and begin to operate inside the streams of power. All of their underlying qualities emerge and are revealed. It's a very good opportunity to test yourself in that way.

Why do I call this area a power vortex? After awhile, you begin to learn to read the landscape. You can look off in front of you and you can see rising and falling ground, mountains, flat prairie, water, lack of water, etc. – you just learn to read it by the signs. In the spiritual world, it's the same thing – reading the particles of space and time, or what we refer to as chit, or chitshakti; it's the scintillating blue light of consciousness, operating in a specific way. In a vortex of power, consciousness has a kind of cohesion to it, like a plasma. It's knit together, and when you deal with one part of it, you deal with all of it.

It's like a moving body of water, that is like a rip tide, like an area of water inside water, where part of it is moving very swiftly out to sea, surrounded by more water. You can feel it – it has a cohesion. If you are in the water next to the rip tide, you experience nothing. Inside the rip tide, you're being swept out to sea, a hundred yards every five seconds. That's how space and time operate in a place of power – it's got a cohesion, it's knit together. And whatever it is, it's going there quickly. It doesn't have a conscience.

Like I said, there are no rulers here. It's just like nature. Which is one of the things that's kind of refreshing about it. It's not ruled by dharma. It has both light and shadow, side by side, all compressed together. It's always very interesting, because when you go to a vortex of energy, it's always populated, even if it looks like the most vacant stretch of desert you ever found. But as soon as your eyes truly open to what is there, you perceive energy and the nature of energy. Energy is attractive, it's magnetic. And anywhere there's a magnetic force, you'll find numbers and numbers of sentient beings of all qualities. Chances are you might be the only human there. There might be 10,000 forms of consciousness that are non-human, yet sentient.

This is right on the edge of Los Angeles. There's a little bit of encroachment, but this area will always protect itself. It'll never really fill in, because power places know how to protect themselves.

The way energy operates in a power vortex is like a doorway. Just like when you are in the ocean, and you're swimming along, the water's fine, then you unexpectedly swim into a rip tide. It's still the same water, but all of a sudden it's acting in a very dangerous and dynamic way. You have to react quickly to save yourself. In other words, it's like a doorway suddenly opening. That's how energy operates inside and around power – everything happens very quickly. It's like nothing is there, then the doorway opens, something whooshes in, and energy changes.

That will be the personality of the retreat these next three days. We will be engaged in the energies of this place. We will be grounding our retreat in the mandala of the Vajra Guru, and drawing on the raw force of this place. Like I said earlier, in the Vajrayana and the yoga tantra, it is very much like swimming – you can't involve yourself in this process without getting wet. It is your consciousness, your being, that is swimming in these streams. The more you understand about yourself, the more you will understand the operations of your being and how the four bodies operate; the physical body of matter, the subtle physical body of life force and kundalini, the causal body of mental formation, and the supra-causal body of pure consciousness. You will come to know more about the nervous system of the subtle physical body: the sensory apparatus in the subtle physical body, the six chakras with the hundred fibers that break out into the 72,000 fibers, all attenuated to the three rivers of ida, pingala, and sushumna, going from the base of the spine to the crown of the head. Also, you will go into the three drops that assemble at the forehead, the throat and the heart, which assemble the world of pure consciousness, the world of energy and the world of formation. Finally, you will explore how the pranas operate; the rising and falling prana/apana, the cyclical revolution of samana prana, the splitting and attracting prana of vayana, and the infusion of udana prana.

These forces are the motility inside the plasma of an energy vortex. If you understand how to use them, it's like the difference between swimming with just your body, or swimming with a large set of fins: your kick is magnified to the tenth and twentieth power, because of the shape of the fins. The understanding of the mechanics of your physical body, and especially your subtle physical body, becomes very important inside the plasma field of a power vortex.

When you are in this kind of vortex, you have the wind at your back, and those spiritual practices that were previously difficult and only generating partial results, will now generate very full and gratifying results with very little effort. This includes all aspects of your practice: accessing the space between the breaths, being able to stop the movement of the left and right channels and merging into the sushumna, moving from the physical body into the subtle physical body, and from the subtle physical body into the mental body.

One of the things that you do that generates a difference in your capability in spiritual life is attracting, storing and integrating power and spiritual energy. The more you have, the higher performance you'll see in the operation of your mind, body and being – your human form. The more power you have, the better results you get. You'll feel the power moving as a pressure inside your system, conducting power through the nadis, the hundred fibers of the six wheels, the thousand fibers of the sahasrar, along the three channels, and also along the formless pathway of mental formation, the causal body. This spiritual power also intensely stimulates the kundalini – power and kundalini are hand and glove.

One of the benefits of this retreat will be a huge deposit of power into the stream of your mind, body, being. Power is responsive to intent. Power is responsive to will. Power is the expression of Divine Will. When your petrol tanks of power are filled, you'll find that power is extremely responsive to your will. This is where the test comes in, because whatever it is that you truly desire and intend to happen will start coming into being. It can very easily turn into a Twilight Zone episode.

It's a funny thing about people. You have will and desire up here on this level, and you know about it. You also have will and desire down here in these so-called subconscious levels that you don't know about. Just because you don't know about it, doesn't mean it doesn't count, which is why it becomes a test how you use power.

You should know that in the spiritual teacher bag, this particular opportunity doesn't come up every day in this way, for obvious reasons. There are responsibilities that come with presenting an opportunity for you to test your wings. You could never access all the power here. You can drink as deeply as you want, completely fill yourself, and still find it to be a deep, endless reservoir.

Inductions of power are very dramatic. And again I say, power responds to the will. You must be aware of what your intention is, because power moves instantaneously. It doesn't have conscience. It's neither good nor evil, it simply is. Power activates the left and right sides of the brain equally, or what we would call the rational and irrational sides – which of course, makes for fantastic dreaming. Our session of dream yoga tonight will be very dynamic, I'm sure.

We are tethering our retreat to the Vajra Guru lineage. It's been my experience that nobody loves power more than they do. You'll never see a wilder bunch of characters. You name it, they've been there. That's why the Siddha path is so immediate – it takes the straight path, like an arrow flies. It's not burdened by the long circumference around. It cuts through – you need only have the ability. I'll say that again: you need only have the ability.

Consider your mind and your human form, and especially consider the architecture of the subtle body. This is where the seats of all the channels and subtle currents, ida, pingala, and sushumna, the hundred fibers of the six chakras, the branches of the 72,000 nadis, the dynamics of the five pranas, all shift subtly in this field. Putting it in more modern terms, spiritual energy and power are magnetic, and attraction and aversion are very powerful tools.

Of course, you understand that in spiritual training, we train ourselves to be neither attracted nor averse to anything, seeing everything as equal. In this way, we get to see things for what they are, without the overlay of prejudice. But perception itself is a quality of attraction; to come into apprehension of a quality is to draw something toward you. Whatever it is that you draw to the forefront with your attention, with your concentration, with your sankalpa, that's what will arise: be it energy, be it love, be it fear.

This is the kind of setting where movement between the planes is very, very easy. A simple tap on the doorway will draw enormous energy into your system – energy that is quite endless. I guess what I'm trying to say is that meditating on power is fun, and like anything that is truly fun, it is also a little dangerous. As in all forms of spiritual dynamics, it's almost impossible to describe with words.

So this sets the stage of what the playbook for our retreat will be these next three days. We'll be in the field of meditation, but power will be a very strong operating principle, and I want you to take advantage of this situation and this opportunity to come to some experience of how power operates.

We're in a very unruled setting. The mandala will provide stability and safety. This area responds very intensely to the dynamics of samadhi. We'll be using the gravitational weight and presence of the supra-conscious states of samadhi to trigger the movement of the stages of the retreat. It's just like swimming in the ocean: if you remember how to keep yourself together, everything's fine. Always adhere to your principles: gravitation, relaxation, breath, the ajapa/japa of the SoHam, the space between the breaths and the presence of the Guru's grace – and everything will go great.

So what we'll be doing next is the generation of the retreat mandala, and "entering as a child." The retreat is generated by an assembly of qualities that I refer to as the mandala. The benefactors are Bhagawan Nityananda and Bhagawan Muktananda, of the Vajra Guru lineage. The mandala is structured externally in the space and supports the space. It is also generated internally. It is the instrument of awakening; it is the instrument of the transmission of Shaktipat.

Once I establish the mandala, then I come around to each one of you personally and introduce you into the mandala. This is called entering as a child. Each participant is introduced into the mandala and to the awakened Vajra assembly. We will be starting with a meditation, and establishing the mandala, both internally and externally, and then I will be going to the puja table and building a mandala, Mount Meru, and honoring the Vajra yoga lineage. It is the magical dynamic of building an offering to an honored guest, creating a special seat. It anchors the mandala physically into the space.

The mandala has a series of rings, from the outermost to the innermost, representing the physical body, subtle physical body, causal, and supra-causal body. I will then be going around and taking each student into the mandala. Again, this is called entering the mandala as a child: the teacher takes each person by the hand and draws them through the gate.

And as I do that, I will be coming around and giving a series of three blessings. First is a blessing of the rice, which I'll be placing on the crown of your head. It is a blessing of the body. It wards off obstacles and calamity. It wards off starvation and illness in this life or any subsequent lifetime. It is a blessing of the body, the vehicle with which dharmic activity is generated. The second blessing will be the blessing of awakening, which is represented by the application of a red dot to the third eye. This is the impulse of Shaktipat. The third blessing is one of protection. I'll be coming around and giving each one of you a protective string. It binds and connects you to the mandala, and in the subtle space of consciousness, it signifies the protection of the Guru lineage. As this is occurring, I want everyone to stay in meditation, and allow each cycle of blessings to complete themselves. This process takes about ninety minutes. (meditation)

Very good, everyone. This completes the opening of the retreat, the generation of the mandala and entering as a child. As we're taking advantage of this place, this medicine wheel, to examine and experience the nature of power and the light of God, I want you to swim deeply in these waters. Use your training to gather and store energy. And also examine within yourself what it means to embrace and come into your own power. There are powerful psychological structures around this idea that you'll find within your nature. There has been powerful conditioning placed within your mind stream, lifetime after lifetime, that subtly keeps you away from embracing and accepting your own power. In this place, in this time, it is a very good opportunity to address this matter.

- afternoon -

In our session this afternoon, we are systematically opening up the structure of the human form. In our morning session, as we generated the mandala and each of us entered as a child, we became deeply connected to the medicine wheel. We experienced how the energy and power of consciousness moves in the creation, and more specifically, how it moves inside our system, the mandala of the human form. As we entered the mandala we became aware of the pressure of consciousness on each of the bodies: the physical body, the subtle physical body, the causal body and the supra-causal body. We especially experienced that pressure along the ladder of the tree of life, the sushumna, ida and pingala, from the base of the spine to the crown of the head, and each of the six wheels, the six chakras, from the forehead, throat, heart, navel, loins, and base of the spine.

There are five basic pranas. They are the prana and apana, the descending and ascending expression of the prana shakti, the samana prana, the cyclical revolution, the vayana prana, or expansion and contraction, and udana prana, the infusion.

Of these five pranas, the most important are the prana and apana, the great descending and ascending light. After that would be the udana, which is the infusion of the light into the form. The human form, the physical body, is essentially a more manifest form of the electricity of the subtle physical body. This is where the three rivers are, the chakras, and all of the branches of the hundred fibers, each leading off from the six lower wheels.

As I said at the beginning of the day, it is impossible to swim in the ocean of consciousness without getting wet. This systematic opening up of the physical body, subtle physical body, causal body, supra-causal body, is very, very important. This opening allows each of us to become completely interactive with the mandala of the medicine wheel, which is the instrument of transmission.

The human form is amazingly complex in its operation. Over the course of your spiritual life, you must come to understand how all of these systems operate and interact with each other. This understanding arises from experience. The study of the human form is essentially watching how consciousness moves and operates inside us. In our case as human beings, we possess the human form, which is one of the most desirable forms. It's highly engineered by the masters of consciousness. It has within its scope the capability of going from a completely mundane condition to a universal condition in the length of a single lifetime. It has that much elasticity built into the design.

As I said this morning, one of the principles of spiritual training and spiritual life is gaining and storing spiritual power, or energy. The human form is an extremely high-performance instrument and operates best at high energy. The first stages of spiritual training are the opening of the system, the kindling of the fire – Shaktipat – and the repair of the system. Oftentimes, by the time a person receives Shaktipat, the human form has undergone a certain amount of abuse – physically, psychologically and structurally – so part of the work of Shaktipat is the repair. It's very akin to repairing an old house that's drafty and open; if the shutters are open, you have to go in and seal up all of the gaps and worn spots. Then you set a fire in the fireplace, and the heat begins to fill the house. If you set the fire first, it just goes up and out all of the drafty holes in the house, and nothing much happens.

So, as I said this morning, the idea of this retreat is to come to this place where there is a very dynamic power vortex, and set the mandala in place. For these three days, I want to simply drench you in spiritual energy and give you the opportunity to see how those energies flow into your system, which is like a vase. But you can also think of the human system like those Russian dolls, where there's one inside the other, inside the other, inside the other – each one getting subtler and subtler. Every time you take the lid off, there's a new one in there. The head is twisted around backwards, and you twist and take another one out.

There are cardinal points of the human form and at the off-angles. Your system is interacting with the streams of the pranas at those points, both internally and externally. If you were looking out from the inside of the circle, you would see these pillars of energy. If you're on the outside of the circle looking in, you also see these pillars of energy. Inside the circle, they're operating inside the sheaths of the four bodies. Outside the circle, they're operating in the plasma of what I refer to as the medicine wheel. They are the points of interconnection with the wheel itself, where the individual plugs into the universal design.

I know how people learn: they learn by doing. They learn by seeing it done, and then trying to do it. That is what is going on in this retreat, and it will be going on for these next seventy-two hours. We'll be operating at high energy, moving the energy through the system. I'll actually be kind of force-feeding energy into the system, pushing that spiritual force into the deepest cavities of being. This will involve the five pranas, the three rivers, the branches of the tree of life that have their deep roots or source in the sahasrar, in the space over the crown of the head.

These forces are generated in two characteristics: solar and lunar. The solar energy is that energy that is dominated by the body. It is brilliant fire-like heat. It's extremely dynamic and explosive, like the sun. But it also has the capacity of drawing the life force inside the body. We can learn to change our identity from the physical shell, which is solar-based, to the internal structure of the tree of life, which is lunar-based. The light of the moon is very cooling. It is also very brilliant and radiant, but the fluids of the body are not dried up by its force. When you get into the deeper structure of the form, you experience the explosion of the ten billion suns; but that explosion – which sounds like it would be extremely destructive

– is conducted along the lunar pathway, so it does not burn.

We all met Gurudev Janglidas in India. The guy is easily in his late eighties, possibly early nineties. He's got the body of a forty-five year old person, and is as flexible as a twelve-year old child, because his entire life force is internalized on the lunar pathway. The ten billion suns are conducted there along these lunar lines.

When you learn to open all those inner circuits – the inner tree of life – no matter how much energy you run through the system, it's not destructive since it is not solar in nature. The solar light itself becomes cool and becomes even more brilliant. It increases into the light of ten billion suns, but it does not incinerate.

The tree of life is actually an inverted tree. The root system is over the crown of the head, and what we would consider the tree, is in this space of our body. This is the dedicated circuitry that draws the light from the ocean of consciousness into the creation. It's as if the body was upside down, and the energy body were right-side up. We think that the head is on top; but in the tree of life, the root system is on top, and the tree goes down. On the physical side, the body goes up, and the head is on top, so it's inverted.

This has everything to do with why we consider and experience everything as great descending and great ascending forces.

When you look at the old diagrams of the yoga tantra, you'll oftentimes see the figure of the human form superimposed over this tree-like structure. In one part, the tree is upside down and the body is right-side up. In the drawing next to it, the body is upside down and the tree is right-side up. These drawings show the equilibrium of the great descending and ascending forces, and the equilibrium of the solar and lunar path. Remember how I mentioned that the movement of power in the medicine wheel is conducted by hot and cold, and light and dark, as well as gravity. This is just a brief expansion of what I meant when I said that there is a very profound spiritual principle involved.

In the first stages of sadhana, as the light of the kundalini, the solar light, is increased, and as it amplifies in the prana, it strikes the body and you experience the Shaktipat as heat. But there's a point where it transforms; it switches pathways, due to the deeper awakening. If you keep the life force moving only on the surface of the solar circuit, the body is subject to that increasing light, and the fluids of life are dissipated by the heat of the sun. This is what we all experience as the aging process. The ability to move and conduct the energy on the deeper and more subtle circuitry gives you the reverse effect. The fluids of the body stay full, the body stays supple and healthy. The light of consciousness can continue to increase, without damage and without incineration.

In the retreat, we are systematically conducting the grace of the Shaktipat transmission into the inner workings of the human form. Allow the energy to move in and act and operate on you very dynamically through the natural movement of the breath, the rising and falling of the prana/apana, the unstruck sound of the ajapa/japa SoHam, the space between the breaths and the relaxation of the body. You'll feel the pressure of it. There will be some stress involved as the energy drives deeper, because it has to displace the samskaric and karmic content that is holding the true life force out of those deeper reservoirs. To do that, it has to transmute it. This is the entire idea behind the transmutation of lead into gold. It's not that the body or the mind is transcended or that something is left behind; rather it is transformed. It is the vitality of the consciousness principle that triggers this transformation.

This is an extremely well-aspected retreat in opportunity, place, and time.

– evening –

It was a very hot day today and a lot has been accomplished. In this session we will be meditating one more time to generate the completion of the first day of the retreat, and then we will go immediately into the second stage of the retreat with instructions for the dream yoga. We will continue to practice straight through the night until sunrise.

The platform for launching into the fourth state will be the sleep-with-dream state, rather than using the waking state as we normally do. The fourth state, Atman, the state of the substrata of all consciousness, equally pervades all of the three relative states. It is very useful to develop the mental agility to become equally adept at direct recognition and contact with the fourth state from all of the relative states of consciousness, not just from the waking state.

It is the fourth state alone that remains constant. The three relative states – waking, sleep-with-dream and deep sleep – wax and wane. The drama of the sleep-with-dream state has the advantage that it is not plugged into the unified dream field of the waking state, which we share as a mass hypnotic state. When we shift into sleep-with-dream state, we shift into a singular mode of perception, using as its basis only the operation of mental formation, the storehouse memory and the sustaining of the life force. The awareness of the senses and the awareness of the body are gone. Thus the potential for moving into the higher empyrean of the clear-light stages is actually easier, as it is not weighted down with the sensory operations, memory, or body consciousness. We have the juxtaposition of the side-by-side comparison of experience.

The fourth state – the advanced spiritual and meditative state of the supra-conscious – is the recognition of reality, which is the mahamudra, the unified blend of the appearance of creation. When we use the waking state as the platform to move into the fourth state, we learn the wisdom of switching the senses off and stopping the mind. We use the magnetism of the body to anchor our consciousness. This is one of the deep principles of Tai Chi, engaging the gravity of time and space and connecting with the gravity of the earth. In that deep grounding sensation, we gain the capability to move into the highest states. Yet when we compare that to using the sleep-with-dream state or the deep sleep state as the founding states, it's a complete change of the formula. In any case, the result is the same.

The mind operates differently in the sleep-with-dream state. The mind tends to dream on a very mundane level, a kind of feedback of the memory data of the sensory operation. When we begin to move up into the higher classes of thought, such as intuition, we engage in what in the West we call the muse. There are fourteen essential muses that are the gateway to intuitive thought. Here the mind begins to operate in an archetypical language with archetypical signs, and even they are distilled into archetypes. The dream objects don't necessarily represent reality as we experience them in the waking state, but are a profound distillation of all of the levels of consciousness – from conscious, to intuitive consciousness, to subconscious, to unconscious and supra-consciousness.

It's easier to understand this state if we understand what intuition is. We know that intuition is the ability to understand something without recourse to the logic of reason. We can use intuition and come up with the right information. Intuition is a compression of a vast storehouse of experience. In other words, the experience of an entire lifetime and of countless lifetimes is compressed down to the size of an atom. All those lifetimes can be compressed and accessed from that intuitive plane of consciousness. It seems like we are making a leap, but we're simply accessing an extremely effective and efficient storehouse of memory, an intuitive database. When things are compressed, they're distilled down to their essence. In other words, they're broken out of the language of paradigm and are compressed into an extremely direct formula or algorithm that doesn't generate recourse to language, but is just essentialized meaning.

This is the basis of consciousness we seek to access in dream yoga. This retreat is dedicated to the experience, understanding, storage and integration of spiritual energy and power. We posit the idea of power at the gateway of the dream yoga. That way, our intuitive understanding of that profound principle can be accessed directly, as dream objects tend to be essentialized expressions of deep intuitive experience. In the same way that one shoots an arrow, it doesn't take very much to launch oneself towards this target. As we move from the waking state to the sleep-with-dream state, we fire past the status of mundane dreaming, the regurgitating of experience stored in the surface memory, and aim our consciousness for the intuitive-consciousness. If you start the dreaming from that basis, then from there it's only a very short step to the direct recognition of the fourth state.

As I said in the earlier part of the day, power is neutral, and it operates in both shadow and light. We all know that our mind operates along a division of the left and right side of the brain – reason and irrationality. Darkness and light are referred to as the unconscious and conscious mind. Power is the great leveler, the great neutralizer.

You either have power, or you don't. If you do, you know how and why you do. If you don't have power, the reason you don't is oftentimes hidden from you, because there are psychological issues that are very complex, such as personal and familial relationships, as well as the way society is structured and coded. We can be forced to walk through doorways that by their very action generate a disempowering influence. Everybody has experienced this. The encoding and conditioning of civilizations is a very direct, very powerful and very brutal operation. It's a dream that every true warrior must awaken to, and often involves looking at and facing challenging issues within yourself. Information about this empowerment and disempowerment becomes available in the dream yoga dynamic.

It's important that you are without judgment as you establish the beginning of the dream. Simply watch what happens. The fabric of the dream is very subtle and it will change; just like going down a road, and noticing how every foot of it has subtle changes in texture and scenery.

Dreams of power tend to have a drama to them, tending toward the extremes of both beauty and fear. They can be extremely frightening. You don't want to allow that part of yourself to become involved; rather you want to stay conscious through every part of the situation, because in this kind of dreaming, you are actually dealing with a kind of healing. The dream itself is a healing act.

We will use the talisman of dream rice as a basis of the dream yoga. This is rice that has been stained with the five colors of the five elixirs, each representing one of the elemental bases of reality: yellow for earth, green for water, red for fire, white for air and blue for ether. The rice has been sitting on the puja since the beginning of the retreat, and is completely saturated with the vibration of the retreat mandala. In this way, it becomes a doorway.

I'll be going around and giving each person a handful of rice. To prepare for the dream yoga, take a quarter of the rice, and spread it in the bed along the axis that aligns with your spine. Take the rest and put it under your pillow where you lay your head. Before you lie down and enter into the dream yoga, sit for a few moments, cycle the breath and move yourself into a meditative state. If you wish the dream yoga to take a specific direction, then set your intention and the natural tendency of the talisman of the rice and the dream yoga will guide your mind into its spontaneously and intuitively-expressed relationship with power – your aspirations, your inspirations, your desires, your accomplishments and your fears will be revealed.

Lie down on your right side. Slightly curve your spine and tuck your knees up slightly so your spine is very relaxed. Tuck your right hand underneath your cheek. Begin to breathe naturally. Reach down underneath your pillow with your secondary attention and feel for the energy field that is carried in the rice. You'll immediately feel it. It'll snag your mental field. You'll feel it connect into the brain. Move the breath very naturally and slowly just like you do when you enter meditation or go to sleep. Then cross over consciously from the waking state to the sleep-with-dream state.

Before you go to sleep give rise to Bodhicitta. It will bring the mind into equilibrium. Equilibrium between the mental field centered in the brain, and the emotional field, centered in the throat and heart, produces a powerful balance of mind that is very self-supportive. It's also useful as the drama of the dreams unfold to stay in equilibrium. Then you don't become so dramatically reactive.

Think of the Guru or a mantra that draws the mind automatically into the higher spheres. If you have a question, hold that in your heart and mind as you cross into the dream state. Oftentimes the very first dream is very dramatic and very explosive, because you have built up all of the power of the day's meditation. Then you'll connect into the mandala of the dream yoga and slingshot to a very high state.

Remember that the night is divided into stages by the natural movement of consciousness, going from the waking state into the sleep-with-dream state, from the sleep-with-dream state into the deep sleep state, from the deep sleep state back into the sleep-with-dream state and from the sleep-with-dream state back into the waking state. Each stage tends to be about two hours apiece. We're all very familiar with the tempo of sleeping and dreaming. You fall asleep and the first set of dreams are very vivid as you enter REM sleep. Then you go into deep sleep state and the mind goes neutral; it thinks of nothing. It doesn't switch off, but it thinks of nothing. This is the deep sleep cycle.

Every time your consciousness changes levels, there will be a drama in the dream yoga. The fabric of dream yoga is very delicate and very responsive. It's best if you have the ability to dream consciously. If you can get into the dream state and then 'wake up' in the dream, and from that place, seek a specific form of dream yoga, you'll most certainly have a very powerful experience. Seek to plunge into the fourth state. Plunge into samadhi or operate in the states of power that you have been experiencing all through the day. But once in the dream, you will be in a disembodied condition. You will not have the weight of the body nor will you have the operation of the senses. It's a purely mental state.

Dream yoga is very powerful and very dramatic. The first set of dreams will tend to be very vivid and have an explosive quality. You'll go through the first set of REM sleep dream and you'll begin to press up to the deep sleep state. As you go into the deep sleep state, you'll enter into that black, void state. As you come out of the deep sleep state, you'll reenter sleep-with-dream. Usually the first two hours are dream sleep, and then through the middle of the night is the deep sleep state. We begin to emerge out of deep sleep somewhere around 3 am. The last set of sleep-with-dream takes place between 3 am and dawn. At this point, the mind has gone through the entire sleep cycle, and the last set of dreams are again very dramatic. They are very vivid and oftentimes the purest.

It's easy to tell when you're in dream yoga, because these dreams have a luminosity to them. They have a different kind of light. After a while, you can comparatively tell the difference between the mundane dream, which is the basic unravelling of subconscious sensory operations stored in the recent and shallow memory, and dream yoga dreams. You want to generate the attempt to get past that recent memory core and get into the deep intuitive field of the mind and into the core of being, because that's where the essential self is structured in the intuitive archetypical mind. Dream yoga is designed to get in contact with that part of the self.

Dream yoga operates on the basic principles of quantum mechanics. The act of perception changes that which is perceived. Consciousness, when perceived by consciousness, changes the nature of consciousness by virtue of the power of its perception. This is the healing power of the deep dreams of dream yoga, when the deeply veiled aspect of being emerges. The dreams can be very dramatic, and there is a kind of integration that comes as a result of them. That's why dream yoga is important. In fact, I would go so far as to say that it is invaluable.

The extent that you can give rise to conscious dreaming from the center of the dream, marks the beginning of intermediate or advanced dream yoga, because then virtually anything is possible in a dream. Like anything else, gaining the knack of becoming conscious inside the fabric of dream is just a matter of practice.

All of the relative states of waking, sleep-with-dream and deep sleep states are dream states. One of the effects of being conscious as you move from dream state to dream state is that you gain direct insight that is supported by experience and perception. The attachment to the waking state as having some kind of reality over the other states is surrendered, and a new sense of reality begins to emerge. It is one of the effects of gaining the ability to be continuously conscious. Again, we have this idea of continuousness – holding the thread of consciousness continuously through the circuit of the states of being, as we traverse the drops of the four states of consciousness.

What I'd like to do now is meditate with you. This meditation will bring to completion the first day of retreat. Inherent in the meditation will be the preparation of your mind to enter the dream yoga. Remember that one of the implicit themes of this retreat is coming into and embracing your power – a deeply personal subject. (meditation)

SUMMER SOLSTICE RETREAT DAY TWO

Good morning, everyone. So we've been in continuous practice now for 24 hours, with the sadhana in the first day of the retreat in the hall, and then the following sadhana with dream yoga. Due to the activity of dream yoga, everyone's dream body has this kind of balloon-like inflation to it, which is very helpful to assimilate the transmission of the retreat. A very large percentage of the assimilation of sadhana takes place in the dream body. You should keep the language of the dreams in your attention field. The language of dream yoga is subtle and very powerful. You'll find that it has layers. When you first end your session, you have the basic memory of the themes of the dreams that occurred in the three sections of the dream yoga session. As you press your attention into them, you'll find that there is an entire subtext of information that is present there, kind of lying encoded inside the dream fabric. I've always found that it is useful to mine that field because certain treasures are discovered and dug up.

We are beginning the second day of the retreat. It is much cooler today, so this morning we will be doing a continuous sitting and walking meditation. During this session, I would like all of you to rest in the breath and generate the SoHam ajapa/japa. Conduct the energy from the crown of the head, through the heart, to the base of the spine. The energy in the morning session tends to have a very full and complete, yet gentle feel to it, similar to Tai Chi. The inter-connectedness between the body, speech and mind, and between heaven and earth is very easily accessed. As we begin, give rise to the Bodhicitta, the platform of the inter-connectedness between the heart and the mind. So in the spirit of retreat, we will plunge right in. (meditation)

As we start the next meditation, I want to give everyone a brief instruction on the Bodhicitta. Yesterday we absorbed an enormous amount of energy, involving the entire tree of life: the fullness of the sushumna and the sahasrar, the space over the crown of the head. In the session this morning, I would like people to press into the Bodhicitta. This will bring about a very deep and resonant equilibrium within the system.

The word Bodhicitta means enlightened mind. It also has a meaning of heart-mind. It is a position of balance between the seat of the brain and the seat of the heart. This part of the subtle body is very important in that the hundred fibers that arise from the six seats all come through the heart, and move up into the brain. The Bodhicitta should be perceived as a singular structure between the architecture of the seat in the heart, the brain and the crown of the head.

The consciousness at the crown of the head is called the white Bodhicitta. It is the form of a drop, which is the essence of consciousness. It sits just above the crown of the head in the place of the udana prana, where the life force merges and blends with the physical body, subtle body, causal body and supra-causal body.

There is a direct channel from the crown of the head down into the heart. The Bodhicitta is found at the base of the breastbone and back just a little bit. When you breathe into the space, you'll experience a very powerful and resonant vibration. It's important to understand that the seat at the crown of the head and the seat at the heart are not two separate points, as in an A/B relationship. They should be conceived of as a singularity. The Bodhicitta is found in the space at the base of the heart region, and it holds the entire heart chakra. The Bodhicitta is one of the anchors of the great descending and ascending light of the prana/apana, which is in the upper heart. The seat of the

Bodhicitta is exactly at the center of the body; in other words, there are three higher chakras, and three lower.

In this retreat, we have been under the duress of a very intense induction of kundalini moving between the crown of the head and the base of the spine. The Bodhicitta is a point of equilibrium, where the energy gathers at the heart, and swells and fills to the space at the base of the spine. It also fills and rises to include the brain and the seat at the crown of the head. As the Bodhicitta develops, you'll find a very beautiful and powerful build-up of warmth and radiant light begins to appear in the heart, spreading in all directions, moving down to include the three lower chakras, and up to the three higher chakras. This will cool the system, and bring it into balance.

In this morning session, we will be passing beyond the fire of the first day: the generation of the mandala, the entering of the mandala as a child, and the intense induction of light. Today, you'll find that by meditating on the Bodhicitta, the entire system cools and comes into balance. You will still be engaging the SoHam and the ajapa/japa, the descending and ascending energy. Those energies will be gathering here at the center, at the heart, and building and culminating at the crown of the head, and building and culminating at the base of the spine.

– afternoon –

I think this was one of the strongest dream yoga sessions that has taken place during a retreat. This observation is made on the basis of how everyone looked last night, and how everyone looked again this morning. It's a very powerful shift and change in everyone. Because of the quality of the dream yoga, I've learned that it takes awhile to get the hang of its speech. Like in all other exercises of consciousness, it happens one of two ways: it happens consciously or it happens unconsciously, but in either event, the trigger occurs.

I made the comment this morning about the registration of the dream yoga in each person's dream body. If I were to describe it, I would say that it becomes inflated with the influx of energy, consciousness and power during the session, which is why I make a point of registering the elements of the dream yoga. It's also important to understand that in dream yoga there is an idea of verbal cognition, a flow of the association and meaning of the words on one level, but there are deeper and subtler forms of language. In these kinds of sessions, including intensives and retreats where you have long morning meditations, you are exposed in depth to a battery of expressions of awakened consciousness. It becomes an opportunity to begin to pick up the internal dialog of spiritual language.

The subtler language, from verbal cognition to pashyanti, is a direct alignment between form and consciousness, which manifests as speech. Pashyanti is a quality of speech that we can become very familiar with when we are around animals. The exact movement, shape and expression of the body is exactly what the animal is thinking. While humans have more layers, and our consciousness is more complex in induction of reason and the physical human form, the dynamic of pashyanti is still an absolute with human beings. It's just a matter of learning to read that language, to understand what is going on around you.

There's still a subtler language of pure awareness, without sign, without form. It is pure recognition. And there are levels of language that you come to have experience of, and learn to participate in, just like any other language.

For the first 24 hours of our retreat we had a massive induction of consciousness in the form of power and light. This occurred both in the waking state of the day session, and in the dream yoga session, while people were in the sleep-with-dream state, and in the sleep cycle. This morning, we meditated in the form of Bodhicitta, which is an alignment of mind and heart. It generated a kind of equilibrium.

Because our systems are still only partially awake, some parts of the mind-body-being matrix are more developed, more cultivated, and more in operation than others. When energy is moving this deeply and quickly, you may get a kind of disequilibrium. So to deal with that, we meditated all morning on the form of the Bodhicitta, the awakened mind-heart, that equilibrates all of the one hundred fibers. The one hundred fibers are the pathways that conduct the forces of life and death. Everything that you experience when you feel yourself to be alive, and everything you experience when you feel yourself drop the body, takes place inside this body that we call the Bodhicitta. It arises as enlightenment, within the essence of being.

We also took advantage of the cool morning hours to have the walking and sitting meditations, which are also very useful. This afternoon, we are going to be meditating again. We're going to be throwing the doorway open to samadhi – so again, it will be a session with the dramatic influx of light and power. We will not be going outside during the high heat of the day, because nobody walks out in the noonday sun but mad dogs and Englishmen. We'll close our session with a walk at the end of the afternoon.

The meditation protocol is simplicity itself: the arising of the ajapa/japa of the SoHam, the cycling of the deep bellows breath, and the relaxation of body, speech and mind. This sets the frame of the four bodies into open and active mode. In this kind of session where there is so clearly a massive induction and transmission of consciousness, it is your job to receive that transmission. There's always a certain amount of pressure. So by staying open and receptive in a positive frame of mind, the incoming flow of light will take place smoothly and with a minimum of discomfort.

When you are sitting in these long sessions, you need to learn how to stay open and relaxed over a duration of time. It's just like running or any other kind of athletic effort: you hit that wall of resistance and you have to learn to actively relax yourself, so that you can push past that wall. The same thing happens in meditation. You come to your walls of resistance, and you feel the mind start to act up and turn into a negative and resistant mode. The body can begin to seize up and become very uncomfortable. You have to use the handle and instruments of the breath, intention and will to keep your system open and relaxed. As long as that occurs, everything will flow beautifully.

We find that the operation in spirituality is not so much a doing, but very much more a not-doing, a kind of getting out of the way. Because consciousness is spontaneous and arising – God dwells within you as you – it is only the realization and recognition of this truth that remains to occur. So we'll be entering the gate of the supra-conscious advanced samadhi states. Oftentimes it feels like a sudden rain.

Again we'll be meditating. We'll be plunging deeper into the supra-conscious, the Nirvikalpa Samadhi. The protocol of the meditation remains the same. The ajapa/japa of the SoHam. You'll find as we begin to move into the supra-conscious, the relativity between one's mind, body, and consciousness becomes less and less a factor, which is an interesting experience and noteworthy. It's one of the natural points of confusion, because it's a genuine shift of paradigm. We are so used to experiencing everything relative to mine and thine, this and that. The supra-conscious condition is essentially the point of consciousness where the relativity ceases to operate. It's what the Buddha was referring to when he said, "If this does not occur, then that does not arise."

– evening –

Good evening friends. The active principle of the retreat has been the light and power of God. Power, the basic thesis of spiritual energy, is one of the key qualities needed for the ability to generate change in your life. This energy can transform the life – kindling, awakening, cultivating and empowering the human form, which is the vehicle of enlightenment, the vehicle of awakening.

The individual incarnation – birth, generation, life, decay and death of a body – is only a glimpse of spiritual transformation. From the standpoint of spirit, it is the life that is to be cultivated, the life that is changed. The thrust and arc of the soul encompasses quite literally countless incarnations, countless births, countless lives and countless deaths. And in each instance of a birth, life and death, you have the appearance of the life.

When you begin to catch a glimpse of the arc of your incarnations, seeing the path of your past incarnations and seeing your future incarnations, you will be stunned at how similar they are. You see subtle changes, but in most cases you recognize yourself instantly. Different cultures, different times, different situations, but there's that same person, that same soul. And that soul is expressing itself through life.

Transformation comes in the ability to perceive the incredible phenomenon of sentient existence, wrestled from its conditions that are given by a thousand conditioning factors: karma, the momentum of action, karma of the mind, karma of the emotional body, karma of the body itself, and the time and place in which the life appears. In each life you see X amount of conditions, some of which give rise to the opportunity of choice, because the amount of opportunity that arises in a given lifetime is to some degree karmically derived.

If you have the opportunity to travel the world, you'll see people born into all kinds of different existences. And you'll often see that those born into extremely fortunate existence have every opportunity given to them. But oftentimes, with such ease given in life, the person doesn't have the power or ability to make use of the opportunities and lives a very destructive life. And those people who are born into intensely challenging conditions, and are faced with lots of challenge, and get used to the idea of difficulty and hardship, live very powerful lives, full of dignity and meaning. It's a complex issue. But it is the life that is changed. And access to power is the factor that gives you the most certain access to transformation and the ability to change your life. That power gives you the capacity to meet the challenges and conditions of life, as well as illuminate the mind, discerning and understanding the very complex, subtle situations of life, and thereby having the ability to make the correct choices.

Power, spiritual energy, spiritual force, and the skill and application of that power, is the key to success in all endeavors of life. The underlying thesis of the retreat is the embracing of one's power, coming into one's power, and having the courage and skill to claim and use that power with skillful means and application.

When coming into power, it can certainly be said that one of the most difficult trials is the ability to express that power with wisdom, maturity, skill and love. We often see the first test of power is when the person has the power to fulfill every desire. This would seem at first like a good thing, a positive thing, almost like a paradise. But we often see if a person only serves themselves with power, they quickly destroy themselves and those around them. So we understand that it takes maturity and skill to use power wisely, which often comes through trial and error.

Embracing and coming into your power becomes a very personal experience because we are conditioned by the experiences of our lives. Your lives are often experienced in terms of victory and defeat, involving the brutal grunt-level battle for supremacy or turf. It's such a common theme in this world. But you also experience the subtle battles for character, morality, and ethics. You develop those qualities or angels of generosity, kindness and selfless service, the ability to act beyond one's own personal desires and needs, and consider the conditions of others. These are almost universally held to be virtues.

To be a human being is to be in a stream of incarnations where you are learning about power. That's why you're human. In virtually every single one of your social interactions, power is a factor. You have to understand it in all its subtlety or you'll be swift-boated. Power is all about being able to perceive a situation and see it correctly, acting with skill and holding the line over sustained activity. Unlike the movies, very few things are decided decisively in the here and now. They are very complex and they unfold in surprising and subtle ways. It takes energy to keep one's attention attuned and on the money, and it takes power to apply one's understanding to skillful action that correctly applies itself to the situation.

More often than not, as you learn about power, you will project the prejudices of your past experiences, victories and defeats across a living, breathing, unfolding situation. And because your prejudices and your past victories and defeats are blanking your vision, you will see the situation slightly askance. That will skew your activity, and you will act inappropriately in a situation. The situation will come unfurled and the desired result will fall apart in your hands. The difference in these kinds of situations is energy and power. But learning to unfurl power like a continuous thread that is constantly present and adjusting takes a lot of energy. Why do things come apart in our lives? Half the time it's because we just ran out of energy – we couldn't pay attention, we couldn't keep up, and it just kind of overwhelmed us. This is how power operates in the basic field of life.

In the supra-conscious field, it is the generation of power that drives evolution. To a certain degree, you can consider the force of time to be one of the dynamics of power. The ability to absorb spiritual force through the instrumentation and structure of the human form can generate an evolutionary change in the architecture of the human form. This is what Shaktipat is, and this is what spiritual awakening is. It's a hyper-driven, hyper-compressed application of the force of evolution specifically applied to the mechanics of your body-mind-spirit matrix.

The process of Shaktipat illuminates the architecture of the human form. Shaktipat means a descent of grace. Grace takes the form of light, and that light transmutes and translates as spiritual power. As it awakens the system, your capabilities begin to become enhanced. Perception and the application of skillful activity begin to correctly align, allowing you to adapt to a constantly unfolding situation.

The impact of light on the human form produces an evolutionary event. Power is, quite literally, like the ocean – you never come to the end of it. To understand what real power is, you have to gain the skill of learning how to access it. The human form is designed to access spiritual power. If you were to look at it with the analysis of an engineer, you would see that the structure is designed to access spiritual energy.

One of the essential forms of training in Hard Light is learning how to access spiritual energy. You learn how to access it, draw it, store it, integrate it and not lose it. Then you learn how to use this energy with wisdom. The theme of this retreat is the light and power of God. The sub-theme of the retreat is embracing and coming into your power. Let's face it

– the opportunity to gain access to power is extremely fortunate and rare, and an extraordinary amount of fun.

The dream yoga on the theme of power produced one of the most dramatic events of dream yoga I've seen in the sangha. This is because it is such a personal subject. So again, I advise you to meditate on your dream yoga. There is personal treasure there. As I said, there is healing in these dreams. The speech of the retreat has been a constant stream of spiritual force, specifically selected to produce a massive influx of energy into all of your systems.

There is confusion about gaining, storing and applying power. You are conditioned up and down the ladder of incarnations by the social structure that I always refer to as The City. You are conditioned by the pressures that you are exposed to as you awaken in the social order and begin to assert yourself. To a certain extent you are protected by the family social unit, and then you must become an individual and find your place. The energies of The City are formidable. If you don't make selections consciously and in a timely way, they are selected for you. What I see in people is that there is a vast and deep storehouse of these kind of events, a collision of the individual with The City. You could start listing them tonight, and we would be here a month from now, still listing them. But you only need to recall your experiences, and even a brief analysis produces very powerful results.

Because that list is so deep and so long, so involved and so complexly intertwined, it is said that there are two paths to the unravelling of those impressions: the slow unravelling knot by knot by means of action, or the wrathful and skillful slash of the sword of discrimination. Alexander the Great slashed the Gordian knot at the gateway to Persia. What a brilliant move! The sword of discrimination is the equivalent of that maneuver in yoga. It is achieved by the stopping of the mind, which is a very powerful reset. It unravels the samskaras and karma content in a single instant and resets to empty. This is the quality of the meditation that we are going to have this evening. It is referred to as mano-nash, the destruction of ideation, which is comprised of the countless cumulative mental impressions, bound by the organs of action, and made more complex by the confusing and conflictive emotions associated with all of them.

Upon making one mistake, you will make the second mistake based on the conditioning of the first mistake. It is human nature. At one point, there has to be a corrective force that comes in and re-tunes the instrument. This is the role of the Guru. This is what the Guru does. Quite frankly, if the Guru didn't exist it would be quite hopeless. You'd never get rid of all of the impressions fast enough, especially because you make so many subtle associations between one thing and another. The fundamental flaw in this equation is the division of a singularity into a multiplicity. The misunderstanding of that singularity as a multiplicity compounds into countless actions that are all based upon that false refuge of misperceiving the singularity as a multiplicity. The associations compound and compound and compound.

The mano-nash – the destruction of ideation and the destruction of the instrument of the perception of difference – is one of the essential tools of the Siddha path, which uses Shaktipat, the sudden awakening, the hyperdrive of evolution, and uses the Kundalini, the energy we call Kali, the binding power of time. It is the release of that binding energy that produces the meaning of compound ideation. The mano-nash eliminates the structure of ideation. When this occurs, the mind goes to default/reset, which is empty. The impressions are eliminated. They can't find their way back again, and the cause of liberation is served. The nature of the meditation is sudden like lightning, irresistible. Ideation is stopped.

SUMMER SOLSTICE RETREAT
DAY THREE

Good morning, everyone. It was an incredible night last night after an incredible day. This is the third day, which culminates in the energy of completion.

The arc of transmission has three clear characteristics. On the first day, we begin with the energy of initiation. The second day is the body of the retreat, when the essential transmission is generated, and is called the generation stage. The third day, the third section is one of completion, the sinking in of the energies of initiation and generation. The completion is the rounding up of the totality of the session, and drawing the highest energies into the vase of the mind-body-being matrix. It is the completion and fulfillment of the retreat. The completion has the characteristics of the highest vibration of energy and the vibration of God – the manifestation of emptiness, as God is beyond all quality, yet infinitely present.

The day is going to be broken up into the morning and afternoon sections. This morning we will be involving ourselves in meditation and Satsang Q and A. I've found that it's always useful to have the opportunity to answer questions that people may have at this point in the retreat, so that the mind is full and satisfied and understands that it is connected to the experience we've been having.

– questions about bodhicitta –

Question: I've heard you talk about Bodhicitta, the white drop at the crown of the head, the red drop at the heart; but every once in awhile, you mention the red drop as having its seat in the navel. Are you talking about the same thing or is there a subtle difference between the red drop at the heart and the red drop at the navel?

Mark: Yes, there is a subtle difference there. The white drop sits at the crown of the head and is drawn to the heart, and the red drop is at the seat of the navel and is drawn to the heart. It is a classic vase meditation where the red and white energies are drawn into equilibrium. The white is the yang energy and also the Ham. The red is the yin energy and the So. The white drop, the white Bodhicitta, is the consciousness principle, and it sits in a kind of vortex at the crown of the head. It is generated by the prana, which is known as the udana. The udana is the energy of infusion and it is the pathway of the light-force into the body. It is the infusion of the light-force that is characterized most dynamically at the crown of the head by the white Bodhicitta and it is a white drop. The drop is like an atmosphere – when you see it internally, it has a subtle drop-like shape. It's not solid. It's almost like a moist gas and it carries within it the essence of the life-force and the Ham energy, the ocean of consciousness. You could almost say it's the first embodiment of the operation of Ham in the body.

The red Bodhicitta is at the navel. It represents the So shakti, and the So shakti represents the manifestation of the creation. It is very elegant in its placement and purpose. The red Bodhicitta is at the navel because this is where the umbilical cord goes into the fetus in the creation of the body, and the life force flows from the mother into the body. All of the manifestations of the body – the various organs, bones, nervous system, endocrine system, brain and skeletal system, flow through the umbilical cord and that produces a red drop at the navel. That is the red Bodhicitta, the force of creation.

When one becomes conscious and aware, both drops are susceptible to movement by the application of attention and will. The capacity of moving the red and white drops changes the universe. You should understand that the red and white drops are ultra-gravity wells. They move in the red and white streams of ida and pingala, and of course they both move in both channels. The seat of the Bodhicitta is a structure that is part of the heart chakra. The heart chakra is very complex. There are easily seventy to a hundred components compressed there. There's a channel that flows through the center of the heart. It looks just like a subtle channel or a canal and it has a preciseness to it. It goes through the center of the heart and it drops very deep. You can feel the seat of the Bodhicitta at the very end of the breast bone, then the width of a finger down. The channel goes down to a kind of reservoir and that is the seat of the Bodhicitta. This is the seat that spontaneously assembles the physical body, the subtle physical body, the causal body, and the supra-causal body.

As the drops begin to move through the magnetism of the kundalini and the awakening of consciousness, your internal and external universes are changed. The movement and manipulation of the red and white drops is employed by the Guru in the generation and acceleration of evolution for the benefit of the student. As the drops move, they produce a profound interrelationship that has an immeasurable impact on the consciousness of the individual.

We've gone through stages in the Hard Light Center where we meditated exclusively on the white Bodhicitta and learned to find it at the crown of the head and draw the white drop into and down the sushumna, straight down through the center of the brain to the throat. Oftentimes what I do is I draw the white drop down and anchor it, where it will funnel into a reservoir. When it hits that reservoir, it's still in the sushumna, but this stretch of the sushumna is very special and very unique – it's called the Bodhicitta.

This is the point where all the fibers merge from all of the six seats and connect at the heart. From the heart, they go up into the brain, and the hundred fibers divide into the 52 wrathful deities that are anchored in the brain, and the 48 pacific deities that are anchored in the heart. This is why they call the Bodhicitta the heart-mind, because the mind alone is a profound perceiver, but not a perfect perceiver. And the heart alone is a profound perceiver, but not a perfect perceiver. But when you blend the heart and the mind together, you have a very profound organ and instrument of perception.

When I say, "Raise Bodhicitta", most of you concentrate your attention in the seat of the heart, and I can feel you feel that curve, that structure, and you feel the rays of that structure flowing outward. It spontaneously captures the hundred fibers, moves up and fills the brain. Remember also that I'm always telling you that the structure between the heart and the brain is a unified field. You should not think of it as point A and point B, but rather that they arise simultaneously. When you get the knack of this, the process of raising Bodhicitta becomes much easier and much smoother. When you conceive of the full gravitational force of both the 52 wrathful and the 48 pacific deities as a unified energy, it provides an extremely powerful magnetic instrument of perception and organization of one's attention within self, within being. Being able to move your attention from the waking state and the physical body into the subtle physical state, from the subtle physical state into the causal state, from the causal to supra-causal, is anchored on the organization of the Bodhicitta. The collective force of the 48 pacific and the 52 wrathful energies gives you the full force of the mass of the brain, the full force of the hundred fibers.

There's an entire ocean of texts called the Vase Tantra. The Vase Tantra is exclusively about the manipulation of the red and white drops, with countless formulas to produce different effects. We use a lot of them in the Hard Light Center. I give the basic instruction on using the red and white drops to focus attention. The drops are difficult to find until you are able to see the subtle body as clearly as you can see your hand in front of your face. Because they're subtle, they're profound. They're like an atom, hiding inside an atmosphere. But when you feel for them, you'll feel them as a gravity well – a very dense form of magnetic energy, almost planetary in weight and infinitely radiant. Even coming into contact with them will yield a very powerful experience. It has an explosive impact on the perceiver. Most people have a swifter aptitude to perceive the white Bodhicitta, because it's at the crown of the head and is at the entry of the spiritual force into the body.

The Shaktipat event takes place in this sphere, because you can capture all four bodies. You can enter the mind-stream in any one of the physical, subtle physical, causal or supra-causal gateways, access the kundalini from that point, and perceive how it spreads from there. But I've found that people have a natural aptitude of awareness from the heart up to the brain, partially because of the structure of the hundred fibers. Remember that everything that you experience takes place in vibrations along these fibers of the 48 pacific and the 52 wrathful energies. They are the Bardo of the embodied condition; they are the Bardo of the disembodied condition, and the vibrational field of the Bodhicitta embodies the interval between the two.

This is why I stress the white Bodhicitta first, because people tend to have a greater aptitude to come into deeply refined subtle perceptions of the energies from the heart to the brain. Because the nature of each of the lower chakras is like a power vortex, they're like massive generators. They're like the big turbines with raw power that comes out of them. The karma they generate has a density to it. And so the process of finding the red Bodhicitta first is a little more difficult. I encourage engaging the white and red Bodhicitta. I give you the organization of the placement, and by all means I encourage experimentation, study and direct experience of the two drops. Find them in their seats. Because of the placement of the white Bodhicitta and our natural aptitude for it, once we gain access to the white Bodhicitta, the red Bodhicitta will come quickly. What you find is that the metaphysics are all based on the structure of the creation. There's no imagination, only direct observation.

Question: Is the channel between the seat of the red drop in the navel up to the heart also a direct channel, a clear route?

Mark: Yes, there is a dedicated circuit from the navel up into the heart. When you're moving a lot of kundalini in the system, it is not hard to feel the gravity of the red Bodhicitta. It's actually extremely dramatic, in terms of its gravity. It burns with the fire of life. It's like a very brilliant, crimson blazon. Moving it about in the sushumna, ida, and pingala is extremely dramatic and very blissful. The sushumna has lots of dedicated sections in it. It's not just a tube that runs from the top to bottom. It does do that in the innermost stream, but remember that each body has a relative fold.

The sushumna is structured like a conch. It's coiling from the outside into the innermost stream, having an open edge. It coils three and a half times. Just like the kundalini at the base of the spine – the coiled serpent at the base of the spine is three and a half turns, which represents the three relative bodies, relative to time. The half-turn at the center is empty, just like a conch. If you look at it, it's perfect geometry, and it coils in. It's open at the top and at the bottom, so there's a stream there. It is often times thought to be a blue, but it is more of a sea green.

Another thing, just a pointer in your experimentation with the perception and attraction of your consciousness to the drops: when you feel for that density of the powerful gravity well of Bodhicitta, it's very useful to use the energies of the five pranas: ascending – prana; descending – apana; cyclical revolution – samana; expansion and contraction –

vayana; and infusion – udana. They are universal forces and are like pillars. It's kind of like using them as an elevator. It can help conduct your attention around your body, where otherwise your concentration may not be quite enough because you're in uncharted country. You don't quite understand the layout of the subtle body. The energies of the pranas are constant, and spontaneously arise from every atom within your being. It's like the force of gravity that pervades the universe – each atom has its own gravity, and it knits together and produces a universal expression of gravity. The pranas are the same way. Every atom has its own prana universe. If something is in the universe, it's because the pranas are manifesting the conducting of light into the envelope of the creation. You can't have the creation without the prana; the prana is the envelope of the creation.

From the standpoint of the creation, the envelope of the visible apparent creation is very small. That's one of the reasons why earth is so attractive, because most of the universe is disembodied. The process of having an envelope of embodiment is an extremely attractive condition – once you understand it, once you get the hang of it. When you don't understand it, it becomes a trap. But once you do understand it, it's an incredibly powerful instrument. This is why we see a constant influx of beings into this very powerful and potent world system.

The distance between the Om point of creation and the OM point of completion is very short. The manipulation of the red and white drops are the foundation of the envelope of the creation. It changes the universe. Nothing is fixed, nothing is solid. Nothing.

Question: When they merge in the heart, do they maintain their identity as white and red, or do they transmute into something else?

Mark: They transmute. The two become one and it's a very powerful alchemy or form of magic. That's where the capacity to change one's nature and evolve into something else instantaneously arises. You don't have to go through the long pathway of the movement of genetics. It arises at the point of consciousness. The genetics just work themselves out at that moment. How it does that is the mystery of consciousness. It's more useful, as well as more accurate to think of the body as the physical extension of the mind. It's amazing how most people are caught up in the phantasmagoria of their incarnation. But here on the retreat, from the first day through the dream yoga to the second morning, a completely different set of people emerged – vaguely similar, but really different.

– questions about death and the bardo –

Question: When you die and you no longer have a physical body, are you dealing with the exact same subtle architecture of the human form as you've described it to us, the sushumna, the chakras, etc? So you just keep working with all that stuff or does something shift when you die?

Mark: It shifts, but it depends. If the person is an advanced yogi, they go into Samadhi. They can enter the condition of death, sheer the body off, and enter into the awakened condition with pretty much the totality of the relative body, the mental body, and the universal body. That is why beings like Muktananda and Bhagawan Nityananda – as an act of freedom – can remain in existence throughout eternity and not merge. You maintain all of the fluidity of the body of light which is infinitely variable and can produce from a thousand to ten thousand different incarnations simultaneously. When that kind of incarnation is operating at full bore it can actually manifest and operate ten thousand physical bodies throughout a world system, or multiple world systems, going through the entire Bardo of life and death, the interval between life and death. It's actually just an interval. The space between embodiment and disembodiment is just a space. Life and death are exactly the same thing with an interval between them. And the conditions of the envelope shift.

The body falls away. That's its karma. It is usually a karmic condition that strikes the body either through an affliction of calamity, disease or decay, and then the life force will recede into increasingly subtle systems. It will go through the elemental systems. All the chakras are based on elemental centers of assembly, of cohesion. Those produce the array of lights that we hear about in the Bardo. They're the various gates. And also "The Great Light of the Billion Suns" appears, which actually enters from the crown of the head. All of the magnetic lights are organized to the various holes of the body. The advice is to ignore all of the lights and merge with the great light.

As you go through that process that system is kind of torn apart through the bardo process. First you go through the specific deities which is where one relives the dynamics of one's life and feels the exact weight and balance of every action. This takes place in the first six days.

On the seventh day comes the judgment. The judgment is, "Do you believe in the body? Do you think you were the Self, or did you really think you were a separate identity?" If you say, "I am a separate identity and I am seeking refuge" – which is the wrong thing to say – then the second stage of the Bardo comes. This is called "The Wrathful Deities", and the wrathful deities come in and they rip you apart. They rip apart the assembly of dearly held life force and the structure of the subtle body, and you are reduced to mind. That's not so bad except that if the mind is disorganized, you don't have any filters. Right now your mind is filtered by the movement of the physical body, and the movement of the subtle physical body and all of the elemental bases. So you don't really notice that every thought arises instantaneously and every thought bears fruit instantaneously. It seems like there's a distance. You have the thought and then there's the illusion of time and then the fruit bears out. That's because you're in the envelope of the physical creation. But as you are extracted from the envelope of physical creation, you come to understand that the mind and the experience of the thought of the mind are exactly the same thing.

Now if you are an organized mind you will shun

the darker and afflictive thoughts and give rise to a powerful organization of mind, and again seek the connection to the great light. But if you are a disorganized mind, you will experience the characterization of the wrathful deities as a time of terror because the mind is seeking refuge, and throwing out every desire of refuge one after another. It's just one trap after another because the mind produces the entire refuge and then you fall into their trap and then they come in and they rip that apart and you're frustrated again and you're driven further down, and driven further down. Every time that happens you're more disorganized, and more terrified. That lasts approximately fourteen to twenty days.

After the end of the twentieth day the third phase of experience begins, which is just pure terror and desolation. You seek any refuge. And this is the beginning of the process of the rebirth and seeking a womb-gate. And so you go through that process and you begin to see all of your future mothers and fathers. A very complex algorithm takes place based on who and what you are, your karmic connection, and the dynamics of what you want, what you were and what you will be. And you're drawn through a womb-gate, and there you hatch and re-enter the world.

Question: When you don't have a body do you breathe?

Mark: There is a mental image just like in the movie "The Matrix" that survives to some extent, but as the mind becomes more disorganized under the constant attack of the wrathful deities, that image changes, and changes, and changes, and changes to the point where you wouldn't recognize yourself because your mind is in a completely desperate state.

Question: So there is not a sense of something like infinite ocean flowing in and out like a universal prana that permeates your existence?

Mark: If you have practiced the SO HAM mantra every day of your life for the last thirty years, you will be organized enough to produce the SO HAM in the Bardo. That alone will produce deliverance. You will merge with the great light. The mantra will draw the great light. It will draw the Guru. The thrall of the Bardo will be shattered. The Guru will basically give you that ten seconds that you need to pull yourself together and he'll just draw you through and out. There is a whole sequence of operations based on how much sadhana you've done and your connection to the Guru. It's very direct, very personal.

Question: Is there an unbroken sense of "I am" through that whole process?

Mark: Well let me put it another way – the reason you meditate every day of your life is so at the moment of your death you'll be able to concentrate and arise as an Enlightened being. If you become super organized you can do it even in this body. This is where that relationship with your spiritual training comes in. Having done it in this body, you've learned to organize yourself for precisely that moment. It's a tricky moment because if you come unglued, you're gonna make a mess for yourself.

Question: Most people don't have the opportunity to control their death process, so does it matter if it's accidental death, degenerative decay or intentional death?

Mark: Yes it matters. Sudden accidental death is much more difficult because it's better to be able to prepare. Again I say, it's a very tricky moment and even though you've trained your whole life, you have to hold the line and not lose your equilibrium when the Vajra army comes for you. And there are a lot of reasons to be upset and to be frightened. When the Great Light appears, it feels like a sun exploding in front of you. If you think it's a nuclear bomb that's going to destroy you, you will turn and run into the Bardo. So you have to remind yourself to embrace that light when it comes. Know it's coming. Know that light is God. Know that light is the Guru.

How death comes is the exact karmic equilibrium of life. When people are driving down the road and they think they're going to work and instead they die in a car accident or a plane wreck or any kind of thing like that where you have very little time to organize yourself – you're plunged into the Bardo; it's violent. You're dealing with the drama of a very violent death and the confusion of the impressions of the death process and the onslaught of the drama can blend themselves and produce an unstable entry into the Bardo. Interestingly enough, in situations of war, you don't expect to live and so when death comes, it's very sudden, but you knew that your chances of living through the situation were not that high. It's a matter of light and some people go through an entire war without getting so much as a scratch. Some people get killed the first couple of weeks they're there. In all levels of those kind of situations, there's a little bit of expectation there.

One of the things about meditation is that you make a friend of the life force. Death doesn't come from out of the sky. Your death is with you every day of your life. Life and death are two sides of the same coin. And if you get very still and look inside yourself, you'll see death there waiting. You can see where it's already present. It often takes on the form of a kind of frozen not-life and everybody that has gone through the aging process to any degree is familiar with that presence. You feel as though a part of the life force is not available to you. It's been taken away from you. As you age, things get taken away from you and that's death talking to you right there. And if you listen closely, there's likely to be a little warning that death is coming. Even if it's just a moment, that's all you need.

The best thing to do when you know you're dying is to sit upright. If your spine is horizontal on the ground, the gravity of the Earth will confuse the passage of the life force through the nerves. The idea of vertical is important. The movement from life into death is the withdrawal of life from the outer extremities coiled into the center. You feel the life force kind of roll up from the feet, up like a tube of toothpaste and enter into the sushumna, ida, pingala, outer nadis and the six gates. Once you get into the sushumna, you just want to fly straight up and out of the crown of your head like a bird through a skylight – as swift as possible, like an arrow. And you'll meet the great light and it will be gone. The great Yogis will always hear it coming and they will immediately just organize themselves and withdraw everything into the sushumna and will merge into Samadhi. They leave one step ahead of death. It's kind of like getting to the front of a mob and looking like you're leading a parade. It's going to happen anyway so you deal with it in a positive way.

Being alone is best. Often times people die surrounded by loved ones and family. It's better to be alone. Your concentration is better but it depends on how you are. Maybe for you it's easier if you are surrounded by all the signs of life, but what it will tend to do is be a distracting moment and you really need all your concentration. It's also important that nobody touch you while you go through the death process because the death process is extremely magnetic and if you're at the exact moment of making subtle and powerful moves within and you're touched externally, the energy goes "zzzzzzz" out to the touch and your attention will be divided in some way. So it's best to just find a moment off by yourself and take care of what you have to take care of. Pick your moment if possible.

Question: I had two friends recently who were ill who chose to self-exit, and I found it very disturbing at first, and yet I understand that they were trying to control their death process and their dignity around that process. Can you comment on that Mark?

Mark: The impact of lingering disease and death is very debilitating to one's concentration, one's spirit and one's power. You need all of your power. In a situation of a long lingering death, you have to consider the force of karma. This death came to you as your karma, thus it represents something that is seeking equilibrium in your life and so, as much as possible, you want to pay all your debts in this life before you move on to the next life. And if some of those produce a difficult setting, that's just a hard debt that came your way.

I believe in the use of drugs to decrease pain. It's not necessary that the person be in pain. It distorts the mind and it distorts the character in an unbelievable way and produces a level of mental exhaustion very quickly. I think death is an extremely personal process.

If you meditate every day of your life, it's not difficult to find how you are connected to the world. The process of Samadhi is really a reflex of the death process. You are drawing your life force into the sushumna and merging into the Great Light through the gateway at the crown of the head. Remember the first day of the (Joshua Tree) retreat we were talking about the tree of life. The roots of the tree are in the crown of the head and the fruit of the tree is the body and the process of the exit is just like a very deep and powerful meditation. So it's better when you are in that situation to simply organize yourself. By the time you get into those final conditions, you are in a full confrontation and communication with death. Death is not without mercy. It is best to exit a decayed body when there is really nothing to stay for. The body's been used, and it is diseased and wrecked. The fact is that the physical body is just the envelope. The subtle physical body is still perfect and so it's better to exit consciously. That can be done with the help of a spiritual teacher, a Guru or Shaman and your own prayers and connection to God.

It's not a matter of judgment. Suicide is not a judgment as in bad or good. It is only addressing the karmic weight of the situation and all karma must be accounted for. If you don't pay it in this life, it will follow you to the next. You might think that if this situation is so advanced now, why don't you just get this karmic bill over with and do the suffering you have to do and then leave. If you don't pay that karmic debt now, it's not like you can escape it. It will follow you. So it's very pragmatic in that way. If you have a connection to spiritual expertise, those kinds of situations can be greatly alleviated. Most certainly all responsible human beings should dedicate a solid portion of their lives to understanding life and thus they will understand their death.

This idea of life and death goes directly to the theme of the Joshua Tree retreat on power and the idea of embracing and coming into one's power. It is your power that dictates the terms of your life and dictates the terms of your death – directly and utterly so. The presence of power is the greatest and most wild-card factor of producing an improvement in your condition – improvement being defined by a minimal of suffering and the greatest amount of efficiency in spiritual work of each life.

Question: I've heard you say that life and death are the same. So when I give in to desires that take me away from the life, or away from the central channel, am I really falling in to those false refuges that the wrathful deities have for me?

Mark: Yes. That is a piece of that trap. That's how the wrathful deities operate. They take the neurotic modes of behavior as natural prey. That's definitely their pathway and access into your psyche. You understand that the wrathful deities are not outside of you, they are your own self. The wrathful deities are those frequencies of consciousness that originate in the mind. They are instantaneous and irresistible because mind is instantaneous. Just to make the point again, if you want to understand your death, look at your life. They're both present at all times.

Question: Earlier you mentioned that if you don't merge with the great light, you'll go through the Bardo, and you'll look for a womb gate. There's a presumption that there's going to be a nervous system for you to inhabit, so you can fulfill those desires you couldn't give up. Will there be a point in time where there will be no fertilized eggs or nervous systems to connect with, and if so, what is the fate of those individuals? Will they have to wait around for life to re-emerge through evolution? Are they the hungry ghosts?

Mark: The question you're posing is documented in the scriptures, that at one point in time the storehouse of souls will be exhausted and life will cease. It's one of the signs of the end of creation. It's not coming soon, but, yes, there is an equivalent there. It's one of the signifiers of the end of a cycle of a world system that the evolution of human beings and potential souls comes to an end. World systems wink in and out of existence all the time.

This is signified by the wrathful Kali that everybody loves and is familiar with, where she's standing on the prone Shiva with garlands of severed arms for her skirt and a garland of severed heads around her neck. The meaning of the severed heads represents the number of times the human race has gone in and out of existence. It's got 108 severed heads, and each one represents one of those times that the human race has ceased to exist and come back into existence. I'm sure the number is much higher, but, yeah, it happens.

– questions about desire –

Question: Can you play with desire in this life time with the idea that you know at that final moment you can say "done, ready to go." Or is that kind of a dangerous game?

Mark: It's a dangerous game because it's fire. Desire is fire, and playing with fire is always dangerous. The formula of spiritual life is always very simple. Simplify the life, withdraw as much as possible – if not totally – from desire. Seek enlightenment. You're trying to strip down the impressions that you are generating because at the moment of death everything surges in. You're acting one way on the outside and you've got all these secret desires on the inside. The secret desires are not going to be secret at the moment of death. They will have their play. And so the idea of spiritual training in life is facing the condition with very clear eyes. That's what is implicit in spiritual training. Usually you see it in people that have gone through enough incarnations that they have begun to spot the pattern. And they are interested in an alternative.

Question: I've noticed that the rate at which the things that you desire present themselves seems to speed up with spiritual training.

Mark: Everything is accelerated.

Question: Is it better to get the desires over with and get them out of your system, or is it better to resist? Do you let the devil have his day, or do you push him deeper back into yourself?

Mark: It's a combination. There are levels of play. This is a question that is responsive to expedient truth, which means that there are levels of truth. There is an ultimate truth, but maybe the ultimate truth is too far outside of one's reach, so that in effect it does not have a meaning or application to the situation. There's an expedient truth where you set the tone of the response in a range where it can be applied. This is an example of that. From the standpoint of the perfect and best results, it's best to throw all desire to the fire immediately. Transmute it into the Vajra-light of recognition, of realization.

Desire is not a thing that's bad, that you get rid of. To use a modern term, desire is essentially a form of neurosis. And at its essence, neurosis is misdirected mental energy. It's mental energy that's gone off its track and is now operating in a destructive way. We see this play of opposites in psychology all the time, where a person will act in a way that's directly opposite their own benefit. It is based on a neurotic gravity inside their psychology, which is seeking to resolve itself. So your energies are going in opposite directions and at cross-purposes. The whole idea of analysis is to try to analyze the rationale behavior with the psychological impetus, and find out where the skew is.

That is also what we're doing all the time in our spiritual life. We're always watching our behavior. Desires are like appetites. The draw of an appetite is not so much the taste of the desire, because if we plunge into it and get it over with and let the devil have his day, that would work, and that would be great. But it doesn't work that way, because desire takes the form of an appetite. While we taste the flavor, we fulfill our desires and taste the appetite of our fulfilled desires. Then what happens? It only assuages the appetite for a very short amount of time, like Chinese food. An hour later, you're hungry again. And the exact same desire reappears, even though you've tasted it and fulfilled that appetite as much as you could. A few more days or a week later, you want to do it again.

That's the difference between a desire and an appetite. The power of a desire and the fulfillment of a desire are not in the taste of the appetite. If they were, then they could be fulfilled by feeding that appetite. The power of an appetite is in its repetition – the fact that we can produce that appetite at will. And this is the basis of addiction. We get attached to the power – the power of the fulfillment of that desire through the provision of appetite. In that moment of fulfillment, there is a kind of power, and the power comes from knowing exactly how to fulfill that appetite. You know exactly how you're going to feel when you produce and fill that appetite. So you feel yourself to be in control.

This is the exact pathway of addiction. "I know how I'm going to feel if I feed this appetite. I'm going to relax. I'm going to feel better." But it will wear off, and then you'll want to produce it again. So the addiction is having the power to repeat the fulfillment of the desire through the pathway of behavior and appetite.

After awhile, an intelligence has to come to bear on the situation so that you can see that the power's coming from the repetition, and that repetition is of the illusion of control. You have to see that you were only in control for so long. Then there was a point where it clearly flipped, and made a pathway or track into the brain mass. You are then being controlled by the desire and by the appetite. Your behavior is ruled – you are addicted.

There are addictions of all kinds, all up and down the ladder, and they all end up being subtly destructive. Because they are misdirected energy and a form of neurosis, mental energy is being tapped away from the river of the life stream. We've all seen a person whose behavior is enslaved to their appetites and addictions, and you see their life force dissipated. The longer it is repeated, the greater the force of the stream.

The answer to the equation is that of the middle way. Extremes weaken the center and eventually pull it apart. We see that extreme behavior at the advanced stages of addiction. Are you capable of seeing the seat of the desire, analyzing the source of the neurotic, misdirected energy of the behavior, and cutting it off in a single act of perception? If you can, that's best. You have to embrace the middle way.

There's an idea of swallowing a little bit of poison to produce the cure. You're playing with fire to do this, but you have to be in a high state of analysis, and bring the behavior, the desire, and the addictive path of the repeated activity into the light. With Shaktipat, you have access to the force of awakening inside the system. If you have a spiritual authority, or what they call a higher power, you can choose to draw the addiction out into the light, and the light illuminates it. It's a very true pathway.

As spiritual beings, we live in a high state of analysis, always analyzing our behavior, tracking down the behavior to its roots and finding the seeds of neurosis that are seeking to be completed and fulfilled. In most cases, when the light strikes the true seed, the seed is extracted from the earth and the neurosis is absorbed back into the life force. In all cases, it is a matter of intention, and the desire to diminish the thrall of behavioral-based activity that is founded on desire. Then that energy can be transmuted and drawn into the central stream of the life force, unmitigated and undiluted.

Question: Is it the desire that's problematic or the attachment to the desire? If it's desire, then how do we function as responsible citizens in the world we live in?

Mark: The attachment comes through the behavior that is induced by the desire. The ability to control your consciousness is one of the fruits of being awakened. You are in increased possession of your faculties, and you can see to the root of your behavior and see the seeds of them. In your daily meditation practice, your universe is illuminated by the light of God, and you can see what your daily work is. The natural tempo of your life will bring challenges that will approach you on your strong side and approach you on your weak side. Everybody tends to do well on the strong side. It's the weak side that is challenging.

The psyche is a structure of weights and balances, of strong and weak, based on the reservoir of your experiences in past lives and in this life. We were talking about how power operates. There are some battles of power that are very physical, very out-in-front, like the grunt-level battle for turf. Those kind of battles you may win and lose, but they don't tend to go to the depth of the soul.

The victories and defeats that really count are of the fabric of heart, of one's morals, one's ethics, and the ability to apply action to what you know to be right. In other words, what you know to be the right thing is the essence of your ethical and moral sense.

One of the most terrible defeats is the collapse and the destruction of an ideal. Maybe you've seen a person have that, or maybe you've had that experience, where you've had an ideal that you've based your entire life on, your pole star, and you come to a point in life where that ideal is betrayed. That particular form of defeat is extremely destructive and produces a wound on the soul that the soul will carry for multiple lifetimes. It will oftentimes affect their behavior in countless ways.

The subtle battles of power are the ones that really count, the battles that you pose with yourself. You know when you've done the wrong thing. You knew it was wrong when you did it. That was a defeat of will, a defeat of morality, of what you held to be true to yourself, so you betrayed yourself. It's always the betrayals of self that produce the most grievous wounds, and everyone has them. Everyone faced those moments, and for some reason, came up short, and a powerful wound was created there. It could be from a previous life. You've gone through the Bardo and come though another womb, and all of that is eliminated from your memory chain, but the presence of a defeat is still stored in the deep psyche.

What you'll see is a person's behavior will sense it, and behave in such a way as to draw it to the surface, trying to bring it into balance again. Usually there will be all kinds of forms of behavioral activity, which try to root it out by producing a similar ideal. You try to give rise to the previous ideal that was betrayed, so that this time you can obliterate that betrayal of yourself by reproducing the ideal and doing it again better. That happens a lot.

Oftentimes when you see that struggle has gone too far, and is over-extended, and there hasn't been a successful resolution, then you'll start to see the more extremely self-destructive forms of behavior, like addiction, and those forms of self-destruction which are like a fighting retreat. You're still in the game, but there's something going on that hasn't resolved. The various scenarios are quite literally endless. But it has to be drawn to the light, it has to be recognized for what it is, and resolution has to occur.

One of the things that people find difficult about

Shaktipat is that because it is of the nature of light, and because Shaktipat is grace, it's tough love all the way. The light will tend to go to those darkest places first, and produce challenges inside the life that bring up some of the most difficult pain. And then you go, "Wait a minute – you mean I'm supposed to feel worse?" It's hard to explain and sometimes hard to accept, but that's often times what's going on. The Shakti will go to that place and begin to draw it out. It's like leeching the poison out of a wound. What I've also seen is that the Shakti is very merciful, in that it won't force you to accept the entire pain of that poison all at once. It will actually be very medical; it will lance and leech it out over degrees, so that you're aware of pain, but it's not unbearable. You're aware of discomfort, you'll feel that energy. When you become psychically awake, you become aware of a very broad array of pressures, outside into the evermore subtle inside. Because the light of God is so pervasive, God is always just going to the next thing to be perfected. What you are good at is applauded and admired, but going to where the weakness is and making that weakness strong is always the most effective use of time in a given life span.

In spiritual life and in meditation, as the light goes in, you come into contact with who and what you are. Part of that is in light and part of that is in shadow.

The part that is in shadow is what is causing the discomfort and the pain. It is the nature of light to dissipate the shadow and make it conscious, so it will tend to begin to draw from those subtle sources of suffering.

It doesn't take long. This is one of the reasons why you are counseled to meditate every day. Bring the life force in and generate the SoHam, so that the entire egg of both light and shadow is illuminated. If you get systematic about meditating every day, you generate a huge volume of spiritual force and power. Then the power says, "OK, now it's time for this piece of the character to come under pressure, and here's this entire array of behaviors that lead back to this particular desire that has been caused by this deep spiritual wound, this form of self-betrayal that happened somewhere along the line."

This is usually where the battle of spirit is fought. Chances are, you will resolve a lot of the pain and suffering you've been carrying for lifetime, after lifetime, after lifetime. Once Shaktipat hits, it will strike that wound and lance it. In the process of the attention being drawn there, you'll come to understand the entire pathway of activity, and the forms of behavior that are trying to heal.

Almost all disease originates in the mind. The mind suffers and the body cries out, manifesting some form of physical "dis-ease." The importance of daily practice and daily connection with the Guru and the SoHam is in this – the generation of a process where the lancing of the inner poison and the drawing out of that poison occurs. The spiritual force that is built up over your daily practice, with your 21,000 breaths being made conscious, can clear a wound that you've been carrying for countless lifetimes within a matter of days or weeks. Some of the fiercest wounds I carried took a year at the most to clear, and then they were gone.

You want to pay attention to the solution, to the medicine. The medicine is the Shaktipat, the grace of the Guru, and the application of the Guru's grace through daily practice and the ajapa/japa of the SoHam. This gives you access to the endless force of spiritual energy, so any particular wound that comes up can be cleared – as long as you don't defend it or try to protect it, which would be a mistake. Simply allow the connection of grace and the force of Shaktipat to come into connection with that. Feed it with the constant attention of the SoHam and daily practice of meditation. Your system will be brought into health very swiftly.

Question: On this question of gaining spiritual power, and then walking the middle path, I'm seeing it as walking the middle path between the intention to will God's Will versus my personal will...

Mark: That's a very good way to put it.

Question: If I contemplate God's will, that seems easy... surrender everything and just go with the flow. But then I think of exercising my personal will, because I have choice in how I want to live this life...

Mark: Yes, that's very important.

Question: You mentioned expedient truth – is part of the way to walk that middle path to allow myself to have the personal choice and desire, but just douse it in the fire of the light of recognition, and then surrender it?

Mark: Yes, if you do that, the desire will disappear in that instant. Part of you holds on to it – God respects free will. God is all about character. It's not hard to awaken a person. What's interesting is the development of the character of people. What choice do they make? What are they interested in? What's the difference between what they say they're interested in and what their action is? It's all about character. So if you make a request, but there's one part of you that's secretly holding the request back, God of course sees that, and the response will be exact. If you genuinely surrender, it will disappear in that instant. That power is there.

Question: Can you say a little bit more about having a lot of fun with all the power, and how to have fun with the power in a responsible way that honors God's will.

Mark: That's a good question. Power is possibility. All possibilities are related to the presence or absence of power. There are different kinds of power. There is the power of the City, which is social power, higher and lower classes, economic power, having a lot or having a little. That's one kind of power. There's also a kind of power that is just sheer force, sheer power. It's like looking at the ocean, and you see all of that force just laying there. Some days the ocean is wrathful with terrible and terrifying storms – that is power. Power operates that way. Sometimes it's quiescent, sometimes it's wrathful and swift. This kind of power is the unseen power of spirit. It is the true power. It is awesome, it is terrifying, and it is exact.

When you get involved with power, everything that you bring to the situation is manifest. So you come to understand who and what you truly are. This is why it's a little bit dangerous, and why you want to have as much training as possible when you come in to more and more access to power. Are you mature enough to handle that power? The ability to arise in a state of power, and operate in a cultivated and mature state of psychology is harder than it looks, because of the infinite possibilities present in power. There are deep challenges to attracting, gaining, storing and integrating power. This is what spiritual training is about, and this has been the basis of this retreat.

The retreat is a gift of power. It's like somebody says, "Here's a million dollars. Do with it what you want." Your character will be tested, because what does that million dollars suddenly represent? The money itself is not interesting. It's what you can do with it that is interesting. Do you take that money and produce a positive force in the lives of others, or do you make it all about yourself? It is the same with power and how it operates, because it puts pressure on every part of your psyche. Your character is truly tested. The drama of spiritual life is in these kind of tests. In tests of power, karma is moving instantaneously. If you gain a lot of power, and generate activities with positive benefit and dharmic activity, you immediately get the impact of the use of that power. If you use that power selfishly, that karma also arises instantaneously, and it will essentially destroy you. When people come into power, you'll often see that they will seem to prosper for awhile. But secretly, they're making one selfish choice after another, and the power is just regulating that, amplifying that, and making it instantaneous. Before very long, you'll just see that they're being overtaken by calamity. The calamity didn't come out of nowhere. It was the fruit of their choices, being driven by power.

When you gain power, you have to understand that it generates the access of complete possibility. So to keep the system open ended you learn to never make it yours. It's like, the ocean is here before you got here, and it's going to be there after you're gone. So if you are swimming in this piece of the ocean and say, "This piece of the ocean is mine"... So what? Power is really endless. If you act in a selfish way around power, it means that you haven't understood something. You think there's only so much, and this is your power and somebody's trying to steal your power.

I have to say another thing, socially speaking. In countless schemes, the city is always trying to get you to surrender your power – your power in the form of time, your power in the form of belief, your power in the form of activity, your power of choice over your own life. You should never allow any being to manipulate you into giving up your power. The very fact that they're trying to do it is a flag. Unless you want to act like a wrathful being and lay a trap for them – that's more complex.

Question: I've been thinking about desire, and it reminds me of the medieval Catholic depiction of the world as a veil of tears, and you just hang tight to your Bible and your God, and hope for heaven rather than hell. On the one hand, there's this magnificence of life, but it's very brutal. The sword of discrimination is a nice metaphor, but it seems to me from what you've been saying, it's life or death.

Mark: It is. The drama of the structure of consciousness and how power is generated is a play between the shadow and light. We have the force of light, but we also have the shadow, the vajra forms of the archetypical energies, of wrath, of rage, of jealousy, of lust, which are all forms of desire that are expressions of mind, and are extremely potent and concentrated. It's not that they're to be transcended. Rather they are to be transmuted, because there's an incredible amount of power there, which is why people are drawn to shadow-based behavior. They sense the power of it. The so-called organized religious approach actually divides a person from their power by saying, "This is hell, don't come anywhere near it, or you'll burn in hell." It's a kind of castration. It's cutting you off from power, because the shadow of a being is very forceful.

With consciousness and Shaktipat, embracing both the light and shadow of a person, you have to be able and willing to be on both sides of the Guru. The syllables *gu* and *ru* mean darkness and light. They are brought together in equilibrium – that's the idea of the Guru Shakti. You are connected. Your light and shadow aspects of being are drawn together, and they are transmuted in that process. There are subtle arguments in religion where this is approved behavior. They control the gate, and they'll cut you off from all of the rasa or juice of the dark motivating energies – along with their pathways.

We understand that the dark energies are forceful, and tend to manifest themselves by producing skewed and neurotic behavior, basically out of immaturity. When brought into connection with power, most beings will usually express the power as a fulfillment of their own anger or through the pathways of anger, jealousy, lust, etc. But that's only because their consciousness is immature. It's possible to be in a state of power and have a mature and cultivated consciousness.

With the Guru, the shadow and light of the creation are equally expressed. The Guru never says that you are cut off from the dark, as if it's bad for you. On the other hand, when you see the position of the religious architecture, they are essentially saying, "We will take responsibility for your soul. In trade for this, you have to cut yourself off from your own power sources, your own shadow play." So they've manipulated you into an agreement-behavior where you will never explore your own depth of being. If you never explore your own depth of being, how are you going to come to an understanding of it, how are you going to change it? So you can see that their agenda is one of mind-control and manipulation, and you shouldn't fall for it. When someone is offering you something for something, more often than not, it's a trap.

Question: I remember that you said the desire for enlightenment was the one good desire.

Mark: It's the best way to use the energy of desire, because it will motivate you through everything you have to do. And it's a lot of material to cover.

Question: I'd like to know more about how to handle desire. I have this idea of dancing with desire as a passionate ecstasy, as a communion with God. Isn't desire a part of God – isn't the devil part of God – isn't everything part of God? I have these desires, and the idea of saying, 'no, you can't have sex', or 'no, you can't do this or that', when I see these beautiful tantric possibilities, and all this beautiful stuff that feels divine to me, playing music, making love – it doesn't sit right with me to say 'this is the devil, this is bad, this is dangerous'. Can I have this wonderful communion with desire and also attain liberation?

Mark: You're talking about the Dionysian path: the seeking of enlightenment through the way of darkness. It can be done. It's extremely chaotic.

Question: Not that I'm going to stay on this path, but I want to feel good and divine about everything that I'm doing. I don't want to have an action and say, "I don't like myself, I'm going away from God, I just did this, I sinned." I'd rather think, "I did this, I loved it, I enjoyed it, it was beautiful, and I'm trying to release desire as a part of my path to liberation."

Mark: What you're talking about are the expressions of the vitalities of life. Again, the answer to that would be the solution of the middle way. Do not allow them to go off into the extremes, either to the left or to the right, because that weakens the center and eventually breaks the center. But hold to the middle through the middle path. Pursue all things in moderation – you'll be alright. As they arise, keep the light of consciousness upon them, and see where they're coming from. If you stay conscious in that way, you can use it as a pathway into self-realization. It's difficult to do because of the nature of behavioral-based appetites. They tend to want to move and expand, exponentially. That's their danger. But the middle way, moderate and balanced, will work. Everything will arise, unfold and fulfill itself, and come into a point of resolution.

As an example of that, among the enlightened sangha there are two basic schools inside the yoga tantra: the yogin lifestyle of moving through life as an individual, or what is called the householder way of life. The yogin lifestyle is along the severe line of constant practice, and what interaction an individual has with the world comes to them through that filter. Janglidas is a perfect example of that; he's been a yogi his entire life, and a huge institution of yogic training has built up around him. He trains seekers who are on the yogic path or on the worldly path of the householder.

The householder pathway is one where marriage, family, and all of the flavors of life are included in the spiritual path. It's understood to be more difficult, because there is a constant arising of distraction and division of one's attention. But on the whole, when you look down the lexicon of enlightened masters, as well as Perfected Masters, it's about half and half. Half of them were householders, half of them were yogis. Both paths are functional. The key to them is that you have to decide what kind of person you are. "Am I a hard-core yogi type, or am I a householder type?" The light will carry in both. The fact is, if a yogi tries to act like a householder he'll be miserable, and if a householder tries to act like a yogi he'll be miserable. So it's important that you intelligently select the path that fits you, because it is the balanced heart that will learn best.

– other questions –

Question: Is Shaktipat just Shaktipat, irregardless of the person that's giving it? I know you said that the Guru is not a person. There's a lot of people that say they give Shaktipat. Is the energy that's transmitted dependent on the person?

Mark: The basic rule is, you want to get Shaktipat from a Guru who was given Shaktipat from a Guru who was given Shaktipat, and that Guru who was given Shaktipat from a Guru who was given Shaktipat. In that case you have the force of the entire lineage supporting the Shaktipat, not just the personal power of the single person that gave it to you. If it's just the single person who is using their spiritual energy to give the Shaktipat, yes, it will be Shaktipat, but it will be limited. It won't be constant and it will have a kind of shallowness to it. The admonition on that subject is to get Shaktipat from a Guru that had the power and authority of the lineage, because that way you have the entire force of the lineage coming through the one. It's not my personal power that generates Shaktipat. It's my personal power to hold the door open for Shaktipat to occur, and it just comes through, like a thunderbolt. In that way, the collective force of the lineage can hold the thunderbolt on to the planet Earth. The commitment to Shaktipat by the Siddha Lineage is ferocious. They'll be operating on Earth on its last day. They'll be the last chopper out of Saigon.

Question: When we've been given the blessing of a Guru, to show us the light and the shadow, at that point...

Mark: There's a kind of protection there. You have the permission to explore the totality of yourself. It's understood that it's a dangerous area, but it has to be resolved. You can go lifetime after lifetime without resolving it, but you can't outlast it. At some point it has to be done. Best do it now.

When I say the lineage generates protection, that's one of the regulating powers. Guru Shakti is a regulating force. It has the cohesion of the Guru Shakti. The light and shadow are a cohesive unity in the Guru Shakti. Once Shaktipat has occurred, the Guru is present on both sides of the coin. This produces a protective effect, especially as long as your relationship to the Guru stays positive. Always keep your relationship to the Guru positive, so that there's a free flow of information, energy and grace, which is essentially an accumulation of all those qualities. The Guru will say up front, this can only be understood by experience. You can read as much philosophy and theory as possible, and you might have a deep understanding of it, but you have to go into the meat of the matter to get the benefit, to get the results. When you look at the structure of sadhana, the kundalini moves through the entire system, and what does she bring up first? The darkest parts of self, the most hidden parts of self – and she draws them into the light, and causes them to change. It's very powerful.

Question: Would you please clarify how you use the

words 'nothingness' and 'everything'?

Mark: The use of the word 'everything' is the absolute emptiness of the ocean of consciousness. And the use of the word 'nothing' is the absolute manifestation of the creation.

Question: That sounds opposite of what I would think ...

Mark: It's counter-intuitive. The creation is in constant shift. The test for truth is whether there's constancy, without change. Only the vast ocean of emptiness does that. The apparent multiplicity of the forms in the world are in constant change. There's not a single molecule that stays the same in the manifest creation, the envelope of creation. So it is said to be the nothing.

Question: Is there an absolute nothing, like before the first twitch of anything happening...

Mark: There's degrees to everything, most certainly. When you set the paradigm by the meaning of verbal cognition, it has a limit. You come to a point where words will cease to operate. Then you go into the intuitive, which is a level of consciousness that has no particular signifier or sign, yet meaning exists. Next, you go into direct consciousness of realization and recognition. Finally you go past that into the para-consciousness of absolute everything, absolute nothing. And you can go on and on and on, but you can never come to the point. However, implicit in this idea is that a single perceiver can never grasp the totality of God. It can't be done. Nobody's ever done it, and probably no one ever will.

Question: When you speak about finding a little, tiny point between the union of Shiva and Shakti, does that have to do with the nothingness?

Mark: Well, I was speaking irrationally, and I was trying to describe something that couldn't be described, if that helps. There's a reality there, but it's irrational.

Question: And the blue pearl, in terms of nothing and everything...

Mark: The blue pearl is the appearance of the universal consciousness to a human being. I think that's how emptiness appeared. The collapse of the mind takes place, and once the mind collapses, what is present? The conception of emptiness arose at that point. It's possible to exist in that condition. The apparatus of consciousness that is the human form can do it.

Question: Is there an example of someone who was a hard-core yogi and following that path, and then they turned a certain age and decided to switch paths successfully?

Mark: Nobody switched, it just arose. Milarepa was a hard-core yogi, and he lived in a cave above the tree lines his entire life. He ate nettles and his skin turned green. He was a Perfected Master. His Guru was also a Perfected Master, who had a wife and four sons. He was Marpa the translator, and he was one of the major forces of bringing the dharma from India to Tibet. He had an extremely fierce personality. He had a few students and all of them became realized. Marpa was his Guru, and Milarepa his signifier. His animal was a vulture, a creature that lives in high, desolate place, just like where he was happy being. So the key is that you have to understand yourself and make that decision intelligently. It will bear fruit, and it will be what you choose for it to be. It's a decision everyone makes.

Part of the question was, "Do people change from one side to the other?" Yes they do. People will oftentimes go through the changing conditions of life, and that will cause a change in their path. We have also seen this with those who have chosen the householder path, as they live through the fulfillment of the householder path. By "householder", we mean those who engaged in raising a family. This is a stage of life, and once the commitment to the family has been fulfilled and the children have been raised and launched into the world, there comes a stage of life called the ashrama phase. This is when a householder will then dedicate the remainder of his or her life to spiritual practices. So people will shift their roles, based on the conditions and their understanding of life.

Very good – very interesting Satsang.

Thank you

– completion –

We are now going to generate the completion of the retreat. The idea of completion is to round up the entire transmission of the retreat, and generate the final blessing of completion. This includes the sealing of the transmission and blessing into each of the vases, or individual participants. We're going to use the recitation of the Six Session Vajra Guru Yoga text The Guru yoga sadhana is an ancient text that describes the nature of the Guru. In this text, each word, each syllable, each line carries the actual form, or corpus of the divine nature of the Guru Shakti. The text describes the Guru in universal form, or the Guru, both in the personal aspect, and universal aspect. It describes the sublime activity of the Guru, the nature of the Guru's appearance, the description of the path, and advice in the process of awakening.

Part of the text deals with the topic of enlightenment and the awakening process. The last half of the text deals with the direct manipulation of the awakened form that the Guru represents. And each line describes a particular movement of consciousness within the inner form of the Guru and the Guru Shakti.

As the text unfolds, the presence of the Guru appears and unfurls. The idea of the sadhana is to listen to the text, capture the meaning of the words and syllables, and give rise to them within yourself. This is the Guru Yoga. By reading or hearing the text and the description of the divine aspect of the Guru Shakti and the Guru nature, by recognizing and understanding it, you can generate that divine experience within yourself. You become like unto the Guru, aligning with the Guru first, and then merging with those principles by giving rise to them and placing them one by one within yourself. In this way, you are transmuted into the essence of the Guru, the Guru's nature and the Guru Shakti. It is a very powerful sadhana, and as each line goes by, the mystery of the Guru's nature is made apparent.

The basic protocol for the generation of the Guru yoga always begins with being open and relaxed in body, speech, and mind. Give rise to Bodhicitta and love of the Guru, and draw the Guru to the crown of your head. In this way, as the vibration of the sadhana unfolds, that vibration of the inner nature of the Guru begins to appear spontaneously in the Guru that is seated at the crown of the head. And as that vibration begins to be generated and increase, a vibration that we call the grace waves of the Guru Shakti begins to flow, descending into the system. There is a direct merging of your individual nature with the nature of the Guru and the Guru Shakti. It takes about an hour to recite. The recitation of the Guru yoga sadhana will be the completion blessing of the retreat.

The Guru is a universal vehicle. As the speech of the retreat is centered in the expression of the light and power of God, the Guru Shakti will manifest in that form.

THE FIRST WEEKLY TALK FOLLOWING THE SUMMER SOLSTICE RETREAT

Good evening everyone. It's good to see you all.

This is of course our first opportunity to sit with each other since the summer retreat. When we were last together we were in Joshua Tree.

This year the Summer Solstice retreat was based on the position of coming into one's own power and embracing power. And in that regard everyone got a genuine drop of The Tiger's Milk. By that I mean a dose of pure energy. The idea of The Tiger's Milk is its essentiality, its purity. It is said to be so pure that a single drop is enough to shatter the container that holds it, if that container is not pure.

In this regard it carried a calculated risk, but based on the level of performance of the Center this past year, and the extraordinary spiritual victory of establishing the ashram, Fire Mountain in Nimboli, it was a risk I was prepared to take. I felt everyone would do well. In that regard that is the essence of the meeting tonight. For me to see you, and you to see me. As you know I am always watching. I may have heard a few creaks of stress and strain, but so far no cracks.

In that regard this evening's main idea is really for you to see me, because I've already seen you. We had a very powerful darshan just last night. All of you were there. How many of you remember it? It is so.

And this is a very powerful illustration of the point of power, and the idea of The Tiger's Milk. This kind of transmission, this kind of empowerment penetrates the length, depth and breadth of the spirit and the architecture of the four bodies – irresistibly so. All of you at this moment look like containers filled to the brim. That's why it's important there be no cracks. In this kind of situation, it is important that you employ your training and your skills, giving rise to skillful means, holding to the discipline, the mindfulness of breath, relaxation of body, speech, and mind, connectedness and groundedness to the Earth, daily meditation, and spiritual practice, contemplation – as well as taking care of business – all of your responsibilities in your daily life. Both sides of the world, both internal, and the invisible spirit and the external apparent creation are involved.

You see, the mind is set up in a form of tiers. We think of them as the waking state, sleep with dream state and deep sleep state, the states that all of us are thoroughly familiar with as we traverse them once every twenty-four hours. And we also have the descriptions of mind that we call the subconscious and unconscious states. We could think of them as six higher subconscious states and six lower unconscious states.

The six higher subconscious states would be what we experience as reverie, or daydreaming and the layers when we go into a reverie state so completely that we seem to lose track of the world. This is what we call a trance state, wherein we operate at two levels simultaneously. Everyone has experienced the situation when you're driving and you start thinking about something in your life and you go into a trance, a state of reverie, and then all of a sudden you're home. And meanwhile you've been thinking about all these things that are going on in your life or something that is going on in a relationship in your life or your work. At the same time you've been driving your car – a very complex mechanical skill, but you haven't been consciously aware of doing it. This is a subconscious trance state that has deeper and deeper levels.

A deeper trance state would be akin to a waking

dream or vision. Also the state of sleep both at the mundane level, and at the deeply intuitive level. The pathway into intuitive mental operations has a kind of trance-like insignia. Last night while you were in the sleep with dream state we all had a very intense contact. You were as present there then as you are here now.

We'll begin to see how the operation of tiered states of subconscious work. It is generated when the attention is split but because we have a proclivity for one level of attention over another, often times the conditions of reality that take place in the subconscious states are almost immediately forgotten after we leave them and go back into the waking state. Now that I am talking about it, some of you may begin to remember the darshan last night.

The deeper subconscious states and unconscious states emerge out of what we call the Vajra energies, the primal energies. The primal ignorance is the creation of, and identification with a separate identity, separate from the Self. This is oftentimes characterized as a kind of primal rage or anger because of the amount of psychic energy employed to generate the state. There are five ancillary primal desires, which are greed, anger, ignorance, conceit and jealousy; they're all subdivisions of the primal ignorance which is necessary to support a false identity.

This becomes interesting because in this past summer retreat, Grace takes the form of the Tiger's Milk, the absolute penetrating pure energy. Pure energy – even the tiniest drop – goes from top to bottom and animates all those levels of consciousness, the familiar subconscious states of waking, reverie, contemplation, trance, concentration, meditation, the various degrees of trance, and the splitting of attention. And we also go deeper into the primal forms, the primal ignorance, the primal desires and primal anger. We talked about this a little bit in the Summer retreat, how the spiritual path, and particularly the directness of the Siddha path, gives you access to the full range of consciousness – the tiers of subconscious attention, and even the tiers of unconscious attention, which are being referred to when the term 'wrathful' is used, and means that the consciousness is coming from that unconscious place.

How can you come into understanding, eventual control, and eventual realization of every part of yourself if you are afraid to open the closet door, go down into the basement and see what's down there. At one point or another it has to be done. Often times you look at the construct of religion and find it is separating you from that situation. We had a long discussion about that on Sunday at the retreat.

The Siddha path is one of immediate and direct attention into the matter. It's a little risky on one side because of its speed and because of its directness. Therefore only certain kinds of people are drawn to it – those with the willingness to bring awareness to all the floors, open the basement door, go down those steps, see what's down there and take responsibility for it.

The theme and the idea of the retreat was the embracing of one's power and the act of coming into one's power, accepting and claiming it. I know the effect of the transmission and the empowerment of the retreat has been enormous pressure trickling down to those tiers of subconscious stuff. There's all kinds of stuff on those shelves. Believe me, I know you. I've been meditating with you for awhile. And what interests me is what you are going to do with that. And not only that, but down even further into the sub-basement and the unconscious primal energies, the primal ignorance, the primal desires, the primal rage. Often times when a person first claims power, what's the first thing we see? They play out their anger. "I finally have enough power to get away with expressing my rage towards the world for every pain I ever experienced." It's very immature. It brings about disaster very quickly. What we're interested in on the Siddha path is a mature and cultivated response to power and empowerment – to bring that force to bear and have it arise as a positive energy in your own life, directed positively, and begin to express that energy positively in the world in the lives of all sentient beings. It's not something that just happens. It has to be willed. It has to be intended. There's often lots of trial and error; it is the ultimate test that really never ends.

Once you begin to understand power and understand that its source arises from within you and that the mechanics of power come from the deepest place, then it becomes a matter of taking the responsibility and having the courage and the ability to express that power and take responsibility for it.

There are lots of subtle tricks because like anything – like love, like consciousness, like awareness – power is oceanic. You never come to the end of it. As much as you use, it's only a drop. And only a drop of pure power can change the planet. Especially if the person operating in that drop of power knows what they're doing. And so it becomes very personal. "What am I to do?" Second question is, "Well, what can you do? What do you know how to do?" Always a good place to start, and expand from there.

It's interesting that the reverberations of pure power are equally banded with all of the fibers of psychology along the tiers of those upper six subconscious terrains, and lower six unconscious tiers. You start to look at what is occupying all these different shelves. You'll find these doses of fear, here, here, here, here, here, here, here, here, spread out and subtly inhibiting the Rising Sun of Love – that pure energy. All of that is the content of samskaras and karma.

Life in all of its complexity has a kind of simplicity to it. I think it's important that we always recognize the fundamental intelligence of folk wisdom. Everybody knows that when you're born, you're born with a destiny, something you're supposed to do in this life, some level of material you are supposed to get through and master – as the direct outcome of your past lives, this is what you were good at, this is what you were bad at. So the strengths will come forward and the weaknesses will come forward and will produce an equation that will seek equilibrium.

As you come into life, you are born into another very complex algorithm that we call the city; the social structure that is waiting for you when you get here. Not only do you have to figure yourself out, you also have to figure the city out. You have to figure yourself out fast enough to define yourself to the city before the city defines you. Timing is everything. It's a proposition that is down to the last second every single time. You have to have a sense of who you are and what you are. And you have to have the courage of that conviction, and the skill to act that conviction out correctly. In that way you'll find your way in the world in terms of being a butcher, a baker, or a candlestick maker – what your path is, and your definition within the social order – what part of the equation you are. Opportunity, social standing, connection to family, access to education – all help you understand the system of the world you live in – all play a part. Some of you might have a hundred enlightened lamas waiting to educate you the second they can find you. And I say good for you. Ninety-nine times out of a hundred it is the school of hard knocks, and it's just the heart and soul of each person that shows what needs to be done.

Once you've gained access to the Guru and gained Grace, that connection is never lost. But the education is in the experience. You have to gain the skill to illuminate all of these tiers of consciousness. You have to learn to live in a condition of love and power, and reject fear. I've watched all of you closely and I know all of you have experienced one of the effects of these past weeks – that the Tiger's Milk has gone down through the system and has put pressure on every part of your life, every part of your psyche and every part of your spirit. You've had many, many snapshots of who and what you are and what you're doing and what you are supposed to be doing. That's the beauty of pure energy. It tests everything it comes into contact with by its very nature. I am very happy to see everyone is doing very well. As I said, I hear the creaks, but no cracks.

All of this comes from the simple idea of coming into one's own power. Embracing and claiming one's power involves so much psychology. The illumination of these tiers of subconscious and unconscious attention is where the rubber meets the road in spiritual life. Know thyself. Or I should say 'Know thyselves'. As a general guideline, when the force of subconscious and deeper unconscious Vajra level energies begin to assert themselves, you'll see primal ignorance, primal rage, anger and the cousins of the six poisons emerge with extraordinary energy and flow into the personality as a form of aggression. As a rule of thumb seek to channel the energy of aggression positively.

The unconscious energies of primal ignorance are called Vajra anger, and arise as a result of the error of seeing your separate identity as real and thereby producing a second thing. Because the sense of a separate identity has no reality, it has to be constantly fed, and this produces an enormous stress on the psyche. This stress is only assuaged with the advent of Samadhi, when the belief in a separate "I" is finally absorbed back into the ocean and the ocean is absorbed into the drop. The overall effect of the primal ignorance, the primal anger, and the six cousins of anger, jealousy, greed, etc. will emerge as forms of psychic aggression and that's the flag. All human beings have this energy. It's not very interesting to become empowered and use the power to express your lower nature.

So what I'm saying is when you feel that aggressive impulse, seek to channel it into the higher pathways. Channel it positively, in positive forms of behavior. Use the systems of yoga and the training of grace of the Guru. We've spoken before about the idea that love doesn't just occur – you have to give rise to it. You'll find that the energy that gives rise to love is a form of will. By taking the energy and aggression of the individual I, and as an act of will giving rise to love, you can very effectively channel that underlying aggression into a positive pathway. This is again something that's very immediate.

The equilibrium between our strengths and weaknesses manifests as the ability to act in concert with the soul and the spirit, or the inability to act in concert with the soul and spirit. In other words it comes out in the form of skillful means. Without exception, to see a person whose actions are in concert with their own soul shows a cultivation that is the fruit of attention to this matter. When a person comes into an empowered condition and that attention has not occurred, you'll tend to see that they'll take the energy of that power and channel it destructively. It would just be a more intense expression of their own rage, and the effect of acting out of concert with one's own destiny.

The ability to read oneself skillfully, "Who am I?" "Why am I here?" "Where am I going?" "For what reason?" You have to have an ability to see yourself; who and what you really are. That's a 'warts and all' proposition. Nobody is all bad. Nobody is all good. But taking responsibility for it has not gone far enough in the human race. It's produced an enormously reckless use of life. The problem with not being able to figure out who you are and what you are and with not generating those actions that are in alignment with your own destiny, is that you will invariably produce rash and destructive actions that will bring about your own downfall. To act out of concert with your own spirit, with your own destiny, with your own nature, takes the form of psychologically destructive states of mind. This produces destruction to one's mind, one's heart and the hearts of others, which invariably takes the form of disease, illness and affliction.

Not successfully defining yourself deeply enough and without enough conviction, leads to finding yourself at odds with the city. It can lead to asocial behavior that ends up in incarceration. You find yourself in violent settings over and over again. In other words there is a cause and effect: the spiritual imbalance and the social imbalance.

This is why I want everyone to raise Bodhicitta every day. Give rise to Love for the sake of Love – so it's present in your heart and your mind – so it begins to sit in the cells of your body. As you rub up against the situations of the world and the city, that energy is there for you. You don't have to take a default position of fear or rage. That energy can be positively shaped like art. One of the dynamics of spiritual training is that the vast volume of the infinite spiritual world begins to open up and move inside you. At the same time you still have all of your responsibilities here in the world and both of those have to be dealt with on a daily basis. This is the Siddha path. This is the Sufi way. It takes power, courage, skill and ability. I believe ability is one of the ultimate forms of Love.

Always remember it happens one of two ways. It happens either consciously or it happens unconsciously. Even if it happens unconsciously it still counts. When we look at all of the spiritual training, in the end what does it amount to? The illumination of what lies beneath. Illumination and transmutation. We see in the teaching stories of all the cultures this idea of the turning of lead into gold, the turning of a poison into an elixir. The purity of The Tiger's Milk is the agency of change.

I always loved that bumper sticker: NO FEAR

What I'd like to do is meditate with you for about forty-five minutes clearing obstacles. Everyone please prepare your seat. Begin the cycling of the SoHam, the deep bellows breath. Give rise to the Bodhicitta. Especially in challenging times, the Bodhicitta is the first and best thing we should turn to. It draws the light of God to the very center of being. Very good, we'll begin. (meditation)

Very good everyone. This has been a post-surgical follow-up. All is well.

Give rise to Love. Give rise to Bodhicitta each day and continue the inquiry and examination of embracing and claiming power. Look into yourself and into the mirror of your own mind. Good night.

THE SECOND WEEKLY TALK FOLLOWING THE SUMMER SOLSTICE RETREAT

For these past weeks since the Summer retreat we've been involved in some very interesting, deep and technical sadhana and spiritual work. Tonight I wanted to pick up where we left off last Thursday in a kind of overview or map of the process; a diagram of the process of the spiritual operations we've been involved in, that have been triggered by the transmission of energy at the Solstice retreat.

We were speaking last week about the framework of consciousness as we are familiar with it, and how consciousness flows through the three states of awareness of the waking, sleep with dream, and deep sleep state. When we add the awakening condition to the framework, we come up with the experience and expression of a fourth state which is one of direct apprehension of the substrata of consciousness. Each of these states has a correlation with the framework of consciousness that we know of as the four bodies: physical body of matter; subtle physical body of energy – the prana shakti and the expression of the elemental force that assembles the continuum of the life-stream; the envelope of the causal body, the body of mental formation; and the fourth body, the supra-causal body, the substrata. The word supra-causal means consciousness before consciousness.

Inside the envelope of the physical body, inside the envelope of matter, and the physical body of energy, intellect and intelligence of mind we have the operations of karma and the purification of that karma. These two processes take place in the sheaths of the physical, subtle physical and causal envelopes. Karma and the purification of that karma occur at all times. The karma is always waxing and waning, either loading on or spooling off and it is doing so inside physical matter and inside subtle-physical energy or life-force.

In the experience of the levels of mind we talk about the waking state; the assembly of reality through the template of the operation of the senses. But we also know that there are tiers of the operation of mind inside the waking state and sleep with dream state, and deep sleep state. It's not just one level and one mode of operation, but there are layers. It's not that we think of it as layers, but rather that we experience it as layers. The waking state is a group consciousness. The sleep with dream state is an individual event –

the assembly and re-assembly of memory, of sensory operations, and their underlying content, the meaning that we apply to our experiences and perceptions. In dream it is not so much that we experience the playing out of memory-based perceptions; when we start to analyze dreams we see that it is the psychological content of the experience of perception that is playing itself out in dream. So it's not just like switching on a tape recorder. What was seen is now being regurgitated in the dream, but the entire play of associations and the interpretation and meaning of those experiences and the emotional tone of them comes through, along with the rumble of memory upon memory and this incredibly complex chain of perceptions that are experienced around the center of any given perception. Often that dream produces a replay of the content of that dream – that's why it will be so much different and you have that incredible sensation of dream where the underlying intention of perception is being reinterpreted in dream.

What we begin to see is that as these layers of consciousness operate we have the waking state, but we also have what we refer to as trance states wherein the experience, even of the waking state, can be classified into different modes of operation. It's classified separately because the mind seems to be operating in a different way, such as reverie, which is like a daydream. On the surface level of the waking state your mind is subtly playing out a dream and you are divided into two places. The mind is divided; part of it is on the surface in the waking state, but part of your mind is operating in dream mode in the waking state. It's operating like a dream. You're associating feeling tones and memory tones, and entire chains of perceptions are being drawn up and kind of unraveled and re-raveled and unraveled and re-raveled. Like remembering a wonderful afternoon with a friend or a lover and you're driving your car physically and you're reliving an event deeply and it's emotionally playing itself out at the same time. Driving is an extremely complicated operation of mind, but you don't have to give it all of your attention. Part of your attention might be in a trance mode.

We see this trance mode go from reverie into a deeper state of contemplation where we begin to penetrate deeper and deeper into a dream state in the waking condition. And we begin to take apart memory-based associations and put them back together almost as a form of inquiry. And we find in this way we can come to understand an experience of a chain of perceptions. "Why did that person act in that way?" "What did she mean when she said that?" "What was that look that I saw?" "What was going on in that person?" You find that you can go into the unseen part of experience in a trance state and operate inside the unseen values. And you can begin to associate and re-associate information that you experienced – the sound of a person's voice, the look in their eyes, the movement of their body, the tone of their voice. But in this trance contemplation state, rather than just the surface play, you are actually perceiving a profoundly complex series of events that are all extremely subtle.

We find when we go into a trance state we begin to take apart our surface perceptions and begin to understand more deeply. On the surface there's a million perceptions, but out of those millions of perceptions maybe the conscious mind just interprets one or two of them. What is really happening as you drop off the conscious state and go into the trance state? You start to go into the subconscious levels of perception. You are beginning to operate at subconscious levels. Perhaps the conscious mind can perceive let's say ten thousand pieces of information in a second, but it consciously acknowledges maybe a hundred of them. But the subconscious mind can observe let's say a hundred thousand pieces of information in a second. And it can consciously acknowledge them – it can actually understand and register all the way up from fifty thousand, to seventy thousand, to eighty thousand, up to a hundred thousand things – but they remain subconscious. The unconscious registers everything, but because it has dropped into the unconscious it requires a process of drawing that information out to access it, and that requires increasingly deeper trance states.

Concentration is a very powerful trance state where you disallow the movement of time. You exclude the operation of the senses and you begin to focus all of your attention upon factor upon factor upon factor and understand them and take them apart. It's like taking apart the mechanics of a watch which has a thousand working parts finely tuned to each other.

When we go into the deeper trance state of dhyana, then the trance state becomes capable of going into the deep subconscious. From the deep subconscious condition of dhyana you can relive an entire scenario at the subconscious level. In an event that lasted maybe five minutes, there were a hundred thousand pieces of information per second going on in. In the deep dhyana state, which is an all-inclusive trance condition, you understand the meaning of every piece of that information.

As that dhyana goes into the deep Samadhi state, which is the fourth state, the mind is transparent like glass in this profound trance. Not only can you see the operations of a single episode, but you can see the chain and sequence of events that flowed out of time into that moment, and the previous chain of cause and effect that may have been set in motion not only in a different time and place in this life but in a different time and place in an entirely different lifetime.

So what we see is that the deeper we go the more conscious we are. But in the unawakened condition we are addicted to the waking state and the experience of the senses. The senses can absorb an enormous amount of information, but only a fraction of that information is actually registered consciously. This generates the need for a subconscious strata and a yet deeper subconscious strata. And we see that as the subconscious goes down, down, down, it is a storehouse of different dynamics of cause and effect which are all desire-based generations and points of resolution.

In the sub-architecture of identity there is generated what is called in the tantra, "The Vajra Condition of Cause". It reduces the entire situation to a primal equation based on the fundamental misconception and misunderstanding of the nature of being, wherein the assembly of the belief of an "I" that has generated the cause of separate identity has put itself in a condition of absolute dynamic stress because it has separated itself from the force of the integrated one. It's constantly under stress to be reabsorbed, so it has to constantly reassert its separate identity. That original impulse is defined as a primal ignorance, a primal misunderstanding. The stress of the constant reinforcement of that primal ignorance generates a primal anger. It's characterized as a Vajra rage that expresses itself in the brothers, and sisters and cousins of the five poisons of greed, anger, ignorance, conceit and jealousy which are all interpretations of identity as a finite condition. The over-arching cause of all these is a super energy that is characterized simply as desire. When we look into any of these particular emotions we see that desire is a piece of it. It's an energy that is an infinite browser. It can attach itself and apply itself in any condition, in any situation.

When you're in the waking state, you're basically running on recent memory and the association chain of experience. And there is always this endless chain of cause and effect, tension and equilibrium, and as it gets rolled under in the subconscious and deeper subconscious levels it is rolled into unconsciousness and forgetfulness. And thus we generate a constant ever-increasing reservoir of content. This happens at an inconceivable level of detail and speed. It's just unbelievable. When you see it, you instantly come into contact with the creation of the universe – all of it arising simultaneously. It's an inconceivable concept. Not only is that content generated from the first moment of the first breath of this life, but of course every moment of every breath of every life that has ever occurred. Thus in any one moment you are meeting the totality.

I also need to throw in at this moment that there is a bicameral split in the structure of the left and right brain. The left brain is linguistically based, language based, uses associative meaning and is ruled by logic. The right brain is formless. It is the part of the brain that operates intuitively. It tends to be more visually based. It captures concept and arch-typical modes. It is the right brain that has the capacity to conceive of eternity. The left brain can never even touch eternity. And thus we see that one of the principles of spiritual life is the activation of the right brain – the activation of the capacity of the brain to conceive of "empty". It is a profound idea. We speak through the left brain about emptiness because the left brain is linguistically based. The idea of the word "empty" instantly produces a paradox in the logic chain of the left brain and becomes a conundrum. But the right brain can conceive of the vast emptiness of eternity – and not just as an understanding; it has the ability to experience it, touch it, and produce an interpretation that the left brain can never make.

I think the human race has existed a long time. It's come into existence and winked out of existence many times. You can have personal memory of having two clearly distinct personalities; a left brain personality and a right brain personality – and we go back and forth between them. In some weird intuitive way the right brain was like a mode of escape from the unrelenting mathematical logic of the left brain. I think the left and right brain have been developed inside the human form for a long time.

You can actually begin to see a chain of disassociative personalities that exist on the right and left side. There are those actions that you generate when you are true to the rules or true to logic, and you do what you know you are supposed to do; and there are those actions you do when part of you breaks out and operates directly as yourself without interpretation. When you watch a person you can see left brain behavior and right brain behavior. And it's more than a little bit of a trick to get them to integrate. It's part of the spiritual training itself, pure and simple.

There's this continuous file of psychological content all the way from the waking state, ruled by the senses, left brain dominant, down to the subconscious and deeper subconscious. And there is a chain of events from the moment of your entrance into this world – when you come through the womb gate – there's pretty much a straight record from that moment on. You flip back and forth into left and right brain and you'll find these two different streams of associative cause and effect. Both are connected to you because they're just the stream.

We find that as we go down through the layers of conscious and subconscious, deeper subconscious and unconscious there are incredible files of experience. Some mundane, some dramatic, some terrifying, some horrific, some paradisiacal, some beautiful. Now all of this exists in a storehouse memory, called the Akashic Record, which is completely open, it's a Universal Library. Everything you've ever been, everything you'll ever be is there.

These are the store house memories of all of your alternate selves, all of the selves that you have ever been are perfectly recorded there. The content of those alter-selves are present and assert themselves as a pressure on the conscious mind – as information that is just raw energy. But it's raw energy that's been interpreted into life force and is a part of your file. It's like constant definition, release and redefinition. Countless alternate selves. From the standpoint of the left brain – the logic based, linguistic based, order of time based mind, things occurred in this way, in this time and in this place. But from the standpoint of eternity, they're happening now, and the right brain experiences them as a constantly arising force without the lens of separation, without the imputed terms of being defined by this time, this place or this event. From the standpoint of eternity, there is no past, present or future. Those are imputed terms based on relativity. But all the energy of these alternate selves, all these different alters, that are in the conscious, subconscious and the unconscious, are all present and asserting themselves upon you.

All of this energy is known by a very familiar term. It is called karma – cause and effect. The intention of each perception, each quality of action, is fully present. Not only that particular action, but its underlying intent – its meaning and its content is present. That's where the energy is, and that's the karma. It's held together by this energy of desire. Think of desire as a glue that takes all of the impressions of a given action. Those impressions are called samskara. They are the bits and bites of data that go into the assembly of any given event. I mean just this moment, there are thirty people sitting quietly in a room talking about this idea of time and space, cause and effect. There are thousands and thousands of bits and bites of data assembling into an impression – the temperature, the sound, just the sense of being in existence, what each person is experiencing, what each person is thinking and feeling. On the waking state that information is walled off to you, but as you go deeper and go into trance state you can go into that mode of experience where the feeling and waves of thought of fellow perceivers speak and can be heard as communication. Otherwise it is stored subconsciously and unconsciously. But the impression is generated.

As I said, the event of the summer retreat is a dose of the Tiger's Milk – pure energy. Its effect is to go from the very top to the very bottom of the vase of stored consciousness. It's as if a bolt of lightning strikes into a deep canyon, and for that split second every crevice and every detail of the canyon is illuminated with brilliant light. That perception causes a very powerful event to occur. It is an instant of profound recognition. Pure energy causes a moment of recognition. Even an instant of that perception is enough to generate a relationship with that entire chain of associative actions, cause and effect, countless samskaras and karmic structures that have assembled into different alternate selves, all of which are present within you as you in this moment.

The movement inside all of you in these past weeks has been so strong because there's been a movement across the board from top to bottom. Now remember one phase is the assembly of karma and the other aspect is the purification of that karma. On the one hand, we talk about production and the generation of karma, cause and effect based action, and on the other hand we talk about cessation – the unwinding of those impressions. One of the skills and seed activities of the Guru is to generate the impulse of cessation, which triggers the unraveling of that karma.

The storehouse of karma of a person is just oceanic, but you should also understand that at each birth you generate a selection of alternate selves that are going to come online and be the primal cause of this incarnation. That selection is pure mysticism. It is the equation between the necessity of the soul, the weight and balance of the soul debt that's been generated both recently and in deep, deep, reservoir and also what we would consider the Ishwara, what we call God, being brought to bear on a given situation. It's like we are all just cells of infinite unity. You know each cell of your body has twelve different chemical reactions it goes through in every twenty-four hour cycle to produce the stability of the cell. And it's the same thing for human beings, the idea that each incarnation is not an immediate readout of the incarnation behind it. It is an equation of these countless alternate selves. Some are positive in the front, some are in the middle in the structural support, some are back in the deep unconscious. But all these alters are assembled and some of them are asserting themselves very profoundly on the identity core, while others are recessive. That is a choice between the need of the individual conditioned soul and God.

The effect of this bolt of pure energy through the system has produced a very profound generation of cessation, but as it goes into cessation it brings karma out of the structure which starts to flow in the bloodstream and it goes through the process of purification. So lots of movement is apparent in the architecture of the psyche at the waking, subconscious, deep subconscious and unconscious states. There may be intense flooding of emotions caused by the swift and deep compression of psychological states. It's almost explosive. Pressure pouring into the system. You'll feel pressure on every cell. You may also have very powerful dream imagery. It has a tremendous effect on the body and on the inner-lining of the psychological architecture.

You know we can also think of the waking, subconscious and unconscious states in relationship to the gunas – the sattvic, rajasic, and tamasic conditions of consciousness. The sattvic energies are the energies of the very high desireless operation of consciousness. The sattvic is energy of the fabric of the great substrata and it's an incredible integration because it's aligned with the substrata. It does not have a desire base of separation. The rajasic energies are cyclical. They are the dynamic heat-based expression of cyclical revolution. The rajasic energies are both the high desireless base of operation and the intense desire based operation. The tamasic is direct desire based activity and is of the energy of centrifugal dispersion. You can see and correlate the energies of the sattvic, rajasic and tamasic conditions to different kinds of states of consciousness and varying levels of trance. The deeper the trance, the more the content of desireless awareness – the ability to perceive directly the substrata and the fourth state.

In the days immediately after the retreat I could feel very powerful alternate selves moving in all of you. Now in this second week it seems as if they're streaming together and beginning to be reduced to a kind of thick stew. Separate definition is being eliminated and the flow of purification is intensified. It's a point of powerful change for the body, prana and mind and the generation of karma and the purification of karma. The envelope of purification is very strong. And it's operating through all of the bodies of physical, subtle physical and mental sheaths – releasing a conscious (recent memory), subconscious (deeper karmic) and unconscious (samskaric) content. The scope of this kind of operation reaches into the depth and breadth of the assembly of the spirit and generates movement. It also generates cessation, which brings about the unraveling and the unspooling of samskaric and karmic data from countless selves, which are assemblies and parts of the content of identity.

As the capability of trance deepens, we can move off the surface of the waking state into reverie and contemplation, into dhyana and finally into samadhi. Then we can begin to see a constant view rather than a snapshot of the canyon in an instant or a glance of the Thunderbolt. The effect of the unspooling of karma and the increasing radiation of energy transforms body, speech and mind. As this happens, rather than living entirely in the waking state, which is the most fleeting condition because it records everything but understands nothing, we begin to live in the deeper trance state, where the direct apprehension of every event is experienced totally, at every level consciously. From this level there is no desire, there is no cause or effect, and thus there is no new karma generated – there is no footprint. In this way you begin to abide in the deep trance state, in the deep fourth state where the mind is operating constantly in that mode in a sustained way because it has moved its platform from being perched and skittering across the surface to sinking into the basis of the true reality which is present within.

When one first begins to do that, the constant presence of all the alternate selves still flood the horizon, so it's a very confusing experience. And thus you are constantly bobbing back to the surface and being hit with an onslaught of the unfoldment of causation, production, and cessation of karma. You feel like you are in a constant turmoil. But as the unspooling of that karma begins to occur it's like clouds are burned away by the sun. The idea of eternity, the idea of emptiness becomes an abiding experience.

This is what I explained at the retreat – everyone here is in a stage of spiritual training called generation stage where you are acquiring spiritual energy. You are learning to embrace the presence of power within yourself and beginning to understand the principles of the application of that power. And as that power carries you into the true basis of your identity, slowly but surely you clear out the content of the unconscious Vajra rage and the brothers and sisters of jealousy, lust, envy, anger, greed – that energy which has generated desire-based behavior from the beginning of time. So as you begin to drop into the deep underlying content of being, your spiritual power does not bring you into direct contact with anger-based karma, nor will your power become involved with that anger or become an expression of anger. You so often times see that in what you would call young souls where the first time a person comes into contact with true power and the ability to express it, nine times out of ten you will see that person expressing anger-based psychology and their actions will be completely informed by it.

So we have this idea of cultivation, clearing and purification of the underlying unconscious substrata of being so that as power builds inside the system you're able to abide in a kind of psychological equilibrium and thus that energy begins to become positively directed and it begins to inform and illuminate the architecture and substructure of being, instead of being just more wrathful and more filled with desire. The inner workings of the subtle body begin to light up – the seventy-two thousand nadis, the hundred fibers and the three rivers of ida, pingala and sushumna. Most people are left brain dominant, logic and sensory based. But as power is stored we gain the illumination of the right brain, which is the part of the brain that gives you the capacity to conceive of eternity; not only conceive of it but experience it directly as timelessness and emptiness.

Why isn't it operating now? Not enough energy in the system. You have to clear out, purify, attain power, gain access to power, store power, come to understand its principles, learn to act inside the rules and principles of power and not waste it. By storing it within, it begins to act dynamically and positively upon your system and illuminate you. That's what I mean by generation: the illumination of the full length of the left and right channel, the sushumna, the seven wheels, the hundred fibers and the four drops, and gaining access into the varying trance states.

The inherent qualification of a trance state is very direct. It's just like learning any kind of training – you come into an understanding of how to hold a trance state. If you can hold your mind in that wavelength of consciousness for three hours without breaking attention then you begin to gain skill in what we call subconscious and unconscious mental operation. As this occurs the curtain goes up and the apprehension of the universe completely changes. What you begin to find is that you've been dealing with a faulty diagram of reality and that diagram comes under constant revision for a phase of time. It's psychologically dramatic. "Oh! Everything I thought was wrong." It's a new basis, a constantly new basis. That's why you need the platform of spiritual training as an understanding, so you can undergo the process. You're given access to spiritual energy, to power, and you have it pour into the system and act upon you and it generates a very powerful movement of purification.

Feel the incoming force, and maintain psychological equilibrium. Integrate and store the power. Direct it positively. In that way by its very nature it changes you. This is the mysterious relationship between God, Guru and Self. And because it is so, it works.

The entire Wheel of Time is an expression of the doctrine of cause and effect, karma, production and cessation. It's the idea of the continuum – that at one end of the spectrum, reality is an infinitely divergent multiplicity, and at the other end of that same spectrum, it's an infinite singularity. That is what is meant by continuum. And at each point along the relative stream of the continuum, time and space operate in a unique way.

Don't know what all this means? Don't believe any of it? All of it is true. It's actually a perfect mantra for the right and left brain.

Tonight we have been speaking in greater detail about the generation and storage of spiritual energy, the process of coming into and embracing one's own power. And how this profound application occurs in relationship to the wheel. The production and cessation of karma. How we arise in a condition of infinity and absolute condensation simultaneously.

There are many stages to the generation stage process. Part of it is sheer mechanics – the unwinding, the unspooling of karmic impressions, brought about through cessation. Then the application of energy and the isolation of energy systems within one's being, filling and illuminating these systems. This is the generation and storing of spiritual energy. Learning to live by the internal principles of power has everything to do with understanding the mechanics of identity – how you arise and why – and understanding the paradox of individual identity and universal identity.

That is the progression of the mastery of trance states – the ability to consciously register deeper and deeper levels of attention. This genuine point of application brings you right back to the discipline and the training – contemplation, concentration and meditation. The relationship of will to action. It is in this relationship that we find the wheel and the impetus of desire. Your action and your speech are constant revelation. The drama of awakening is under constant pressure of revelation. What you hold to be true is constantly washed away, restructured, washed away and restructured. It's like constantly receiving a more detailed map.

Tonight our cause has been advanced very well.

Sadgurunath Maharaj Ki Jai

Good Night.

THE THIRD WEEKLY TALK FOLLOWING THE SUMMER SOLSTICE RETREAT

This has been a very dynamic summer. I am very happy with how the spiritual work is moving apace and especially as it is unfolding inside the sangha, both as a group and with each of you individually. We're still very much inside the wave that was set in motion at the Summer retreat. A blow like that moves very swiftly to the very depths and unfolds and generates fortune after fortune of Grace Waves. Coming into direct contact with the source of infinite power, and being brought into alignment with that, sets in motion seeds that will continue to ripen. Coming into one's own power generates a constant purification, and with purification comes a constant clarification. It brings the emergence of an inner ideal which is the expression of the spontaneously born enlightenment. It is the coming to terms with this idea, the true great work of all life that is of which we speak.

As awakening ripens within a person we will often see that the cultivation of the ideal of enlightenment is purified and clarified as it becomes more centralized. This ideal of enlightenment is the true source of all desire and action. In an unripened condition we often will see stand-in desires or avataric representations of that enlightenment ideal, such as the desire for love, or the desire for power or for various kinds of experience. But as that cultivation sharpens and intensifies, the matter becomes more direct and becomes the issue of awakening and of enlightenment itself.

As this occurs there is also what we would call The Path With Heart. We look at what the predisposition of a person's nature is. What are their inherent skills? What are their capabilities? What is the nature of their soul debt? Because as we always come to find out, enlightenment takes place inside life itself. And life is essentially about that experience that arises from action. What do we love? Because it's what we love that we commit ourselves to. Are we willing to withstand the challenges and difficulties that emerge in the arising of an ideal as it meets the world through our action? The nature of our voice arises in our ability, and thus we see this relationship of the ideal of enlightenment and the relationship of Iccha, the power of will and its two-fold nature of individual will and Divine Will. Individual will is the speech of the individual, the voice of ability, the voice of constant purification and clarification of identity; Divine Will is the great force and the great speech of the SoHam – the arising of the Ocean and the expression of the infinite creation.

That relationship of desire and the application of will to that desire gives rise to action. As we become more experienced we come to see the genuine difficulty in generating true accomplishment; the skillful application of oneself to the expression and speech of one's individual desire, and bringing individual will coming into relationship with the mystery of the Universal and Divine Will. Learning to express what is necessary to generate the ideal of enlightenment in pure action and skillful means is power. The momentum of this movement from the Joshua Tree Summer retreat and its expression as the Grace Waves of power are not even beginning to abate. In fact they are picking up strength and moving into greater depth.

And so this evening, what I wanted to do is address the application of our awareness, of our lives, to this swiftly moving wave, that is invisibly moving with incredible force inside the life stream. Always remember: it is the life that is cultivated. It is the life that changes. The body comes and goes as we move in and out of this envelope of the creation. The body falls away but the mind essence, which carries the bill of lading and content of experiences, migrates from lifetime to lifetime. The content of each life is a constant re-negotiation of those qualities.

As we were recently talking about, it is not necessarily true that every single quality from every single life reincarnates into the next given life. At the moment of birth there is an arrangement made between the Creator and the conditioned soul about what qualities are going to be brought to bear. Oftentimes when you regard the qualities of your incarnation they will actually be a balanced or semi-balanced list of strengths and weaknesses – areas of incumbent strength and areas of newly applied challenges that will bring about new strengths but are presently undeveloped. You need the basic strengths as your foundation, but if we were to cast God as a teacher he would say, "Well yes, you were very good at this, but there's this set of qualities over here that has not been convincingly cultivated, so let's throw that into the mix."

We have this challenge posed to us about how sophisticated our view is. Are we still watching the light glint off the surface of things? Do we believe the report of our senses and call that reality? Or have we begun to experience things in enough depth that we know to look past that surface phantasmagoria into the deeper inner workings – and to what extent? This is always a matter of experience, and this is the essence of the skillful means – the ability to read the underlying truth of a thing while ignoring its apparent appearance. Things are rarely what they appear to be.

The origins of a being are obscure. The spirit is deeply veiled. This is the question of the ages and the question that is posed to a human being every time they're born, "What are you interested in? Where do you come from? Where are you going?" This situation is always a matter of experience. It is not a matter of philosophy. Philosophical thought is an encoded template. It can be useful – in fact is very useful. It's like a tool. You have to know how to use it.

What I wanted to do with you tonight is a session of what I would call Power Bodhicitta. As we know, the word Bodhicitta means awakened mind and has as its subtitle the "heart-mind-matrix". It is based on the hundred fibers: the forty-eight peaceful deities or energies that originate in the heart center and the fifty-two wrathful deities that originate in the mind. Inherent in this structure is the idea that the heart alone is an imperfect perceiver and the mind alone is an imperfect perceiver; but blending the two together produces a very powerful platform of integration and illuminates the entire structure.

I also want to remind you that in yogic anatomy, the structure of the heart terminates in the crown of the head, and the sahasrar and the heart are a single structure. They are not two structures that are bound together but are so unified that they should be considered to be a single piece of spiritual architecture. The activation of the center at the heart – an extremely complex center – gives you complete control of the pranas, the three rivers and the crown of the head. This gives you complete access to the sahasrar and the upper spheres of consciousness that are the basis of the supra-conscious states. It connects you to the super power of the supra-conscious, and at the same time allows you to hold on and establish a connection to the physical body.

There is an extreme dynamic tension between Ham – the structure of being which is formless and of the nature of the ocean, and the vibration of the syllable So, which is the expression of the creation. As I've said many times, on the Siddha path, we don't embrace or approach things from a philosophical or abstract point of view. The identity, the concept of self is completely articulated inside the experience.

It will be deleterious to the realization if you project enlightenment as somewhere beyond yourself or as some quality of abstraction that is to be considered, constructed or projected. When you place the framework of the incredible depth and breadth of consciousness that is expressed in the SoHam within you as you, when you place it all around you as you, then it begins to operate as it is meant to operate. It will assert an extraordinary impact upon your system. Consciousness has a force to it that will blow through the architecture of the four bodies like a hurricane.

So in that spirit what I want to do is plunge into the Bodhicitta in a power format. When navigating tempestuous waters in your life and in your sadhana, the Bodhicitta is the absolute, fail safe, go to position of consciousness. It will integrate you deeply at the level of awakened heart and awakened mind, the entire architecture of the four bodies and the SoHam. The infinite ocean and the infinite creation. It lends completely dynamic and functional stability in absolutely any situation. When you are moving in intense waters of purification and clarification you should generate the Bodhicitta daily. It will clarify and purify afflictive emotion, confusion, unclear views and misunderstandings. It will lend clarity to any situation. It also kindles the angels of love, generosity, kindness, patience, and lights the lamp of courage in the heart.

The seat of the Bodhicitta is in the heart region. In the deep heart at the base of the sternum and back towards the center of the body there is a celestial akasha – a divine space. You can feel that it's almost like a thermometer, a very fine stream that goes down to the deep and opens up into a well. You don't have to create it with your mind. It's already there. In this space, the spontaneously arising vibration of enlightenment is present.

As we begin, everyone please begin cycling the deep bellow's breath, deeply and slowly. It is especially important at the beginning to very physically embrace the bellow's breath. In other words, really use the bellows of the diaphragm because it will very much open up the front of the body and the back of the body. You'll feel all of the streams and nadis in the physical body of the microcosmic orbit. And you'll begin to feel very distinctly the simultaneously descending and ascending energies that meet at the heart. Again listen to the SoHam. We'll begin. (meditation).

This way of meditating on the Bodhicitta is a form of Vase sadhana, where the energies and polarities, the polar opposites, are brought into a point of equilibrium with the heart-mind. The understanding and mastery of the red and white energies in relationship to the three rivers – the vital channels of the ida, pingala and sushumna – and all the subtle ancillary nadis which are the pathways of the karma-producing winds, which are the vase – the relationship of the spiritual energies with the envelopes of the four bodies.

By bringing the red and white energies to a point of focus in the Bodhicitta, you can deliberately drive that energy into the karma-producing channels, capture them, and make them of one flavor. By stopping them and drawing them into the center, the forces of the cycling of life and death are brought to a point. This also draws energy to the center. The seat of the Bodhicitta, the seat of the heart, is the center of the human form: three higher and three lower planes in almost total equilibrium. After this exercise, as you cycle the SoHam, you'll find a very large reservoir of energy at the center of the rising and falling energy. You'll find the space of emptiness and the space between the breaths dramatically amplified.

This is one of the kinds of meditations that really benefits from duration, because you're quite literally pressing the electrical force of the creation through the formation. As it goes through, it purifies and clarifies, and all of the hemispheres of the human form become very clearly articulated. Speaking of the descending and ascending energies of front and back, left and right, red and white, you'll find a very sharp division begin to form at the cardinal points and at the diagonal points. The pranas are constantly flowing along those channels and are articulating the true shape of the egg, drawing the energy up from the Earth with the force of the Kundalini and the descending force of the ocean, the white drop, all aligning at the heart. You bring the great polarity of SoHam to the very center of being. You're knit at the center and this provides a very powerful, magnetic adhesion to the formation of being. It becomes easier to become grounded and have a clear, resonant vibration. You begin to spontaneously throw off the vibrations of afflictive emotion and mental confusion.

Pay attention to this idea of merging the So and Ham at the seat of the heart, at the Bodhicitta. It becomes a very tight knit orbit and you'll feel it producing this constant and ever shifting equilibrium as the magnetic force of the Bodhicitta begins to capture more and more of the physical, subtle physical and causal bodies. It starts to reach out and catch different sections of ida, pingala and sushumna, and then the hundred fibers, and then the seventy-six thousand subtle fibers in which the incredibly subtle algorithm of your karma is quite literally written. By overwhelming it with the force of the Bodhicitta you turn it into one flavor and draw it to the central channel, and those cyclical karmic energies are consumed.

As you sit in this mode for hours and days it has a very intensely accumulative magnetic force and will quite literally begin to bend reality.

I also want to draw your attention to the method of bringing the focus into the heart region and then releasing that concentration, so it spreads and captures the entire length of the sushumna. It's a very dramatic movement of attention. So in this way, we get the benefit of the Bodhicitta along with the amplification of bringing the polar opposites into equilibrium with focus, and moving through the envelope of the four bodies.

Very good everyone.

Good night.

WHAT IS HERE IS EVERYWHERE INTENSIVE
JULY 19, 2008

I would like to welcome you all with love to the Guru Purnima Intensive. This is the completion of an extraordinary week of dharma, where we've had the opportunity to be together five out of the past ten days. In that regard, the spiritual force aroused for the intensive is already very much moving at full force. As such, we don't really need a building-up period. So I would very much like to plunge right into the essence of the intensive.

In the spirit of the day, I would like to share with you one of the secrets of the Siddhas, one of the secrets of the yoga tantra, one of the secrets of the gurus. As such, it is an old idea, and it is very simple. It goes something like this: what is here is everywhere; and what is not here is nowhere. It is to say that absolutely everything, everything in existence, everything outside of existence, in all terms – everything – even nothingness itself, emptiness, is here. It is a powerful idea, and it is so. Nothing can come into existence, even the absolute void of existence, without being connected to everything else. There is not and has never been a second thing. This is what the Siddhas and the sages discovered. To see everything, you seek here; and thus, it will appear.

As we are sitting in celebration of the universal teacher, this Vyasa Purnima, I feel it is important that we base our celebration on the pointing out of an essential truth, one single truth that leads to everything. What is here is everywhere, what is not here, is nowhere.

Today we are celebrating the universal teacher, the Guru; that which arises, that which incarnates to reveal the truth. Arising everywhere, it is revealed, realized and recognized here. I've spoken to you of the mechanics of the structure of the human form. Inherent in the architecture of the human form there is a superstructure, a triangle-like shape, that is seated at the crown of the head just underneath the brahmarandhra. You would consider it to be in the physical body and part of the cells of the cerebrum, the brain mass that is responsible for the highest brain functions. It has been found in the physical body as a triangular set of cells in the cerebrum.

It also exists in the subtle physical body at the very

top of the sushumna, but inside the contour of the human body. In other words, it's underneath the skull. The sushumna moves from the base of the spine up through the brain, up to the space at the crown of the head, into the space over the crown of the head. The architecture of the sushumna is like an antenna that is designed to capture and express the vibration of all the worlds of the creation. In other words, everyone and everything is inside sushumna. The arc of your incarnations take place as the movement in sushumna and in the manipulation of the subtle, phenomenal points of consciousness that are attenuated to sushumna.

There is a dazzling array of instruments of consciousness dedicated to conducting the supra-conscious, at an incredible velocity and at an incredible level of energy, from the space over the crown of the head, to the crown of the head, down through the six chakras, into the root and through the root down into the earth. This triangular shape at the top of the sushumna is a part of the architecture of the sahasrar, and is the interface between the crown of the head and below, and the space over the crown of the head and above.

Loosely speaking, from the crown of the head down, the vibration is said to be inside the order of the wheel of time; in the space over the crown of the head, it is in a kind of supra-reality that is outside of time, and is eternal and without change. It is in this movement of consciousness up and down sushumna where the operation of time is relative, that we begin to see the idea of past, present and future. And we also see that idea of three times and thus three places, is a relative perception.

Consider this array of instrumentation, designed to experience consciousness at every level of the spectrum: at one end of the antenna, we experience the vibration of consciousness in its eternal, unchanging nature. We refer to this vibration as the HAM syllable. From the point of the crown of the head, down through the center of the body, anchoring into the root and down into the earth, we have its opposite spectrum, where consciousness is expressed as constant multiplicity and is in constant transient change. We experience consciousness in this way as the creation, and its vibration is the syllable SO.

Visualize the sushumna as an antenna array – three and a half feet, from the base of the spine to the crown of the head, three and a half feet from the crown of the head up into the space over the crown of the head. What is at the exact dead center? It is this triangular shape. It's entire function is to expresses the vibration of the guru and the guru shakti. It's like a vajra, a fulcrum.

With each breath we breathe, the syllable HAM begins vibrating at the crown of the head and sinks down through the sushumna, ida and pingala, all of the relative pathways, into its base at the root. At the other end of the aspiration, the syllable SO vibrates at the base of the spine, vibrates up the pathway, ida, pingala and sushumna, rising up and spreading out. Thus we feel a constant, integrated and interconnected flow. Everything that is in existence, even including the concept of non-existence, which is a form of existence, even the sub-strata of Atman and the sub-sub-strata of emptiness is conducted along this antenna of sushumna. With every cycle of breath, with every aspiration, every in-and-out breath, the vibration of the HAM, which is the true everything, vibrates through the antenna of sushumna, into the arising appearance of the creation, which is the true nothing. From the standpoint of everything, even nothing is a part of it.

The yoga tantrica and the siddhas have a knack for understating things and stating the most profound ideas in the simplest way – so simple that you're likely to overlook it. And thus they say: everything is here. Awareness, the mind, the engine of perception, has no qualities of its own. It is like a mirror. What does a mirror do? It does one thing: it reflects what it comes into contact with. But is it ever the thing itself? No, it's a reflection of it, constantly changing.

There's a concept in art that form is function. Just look at the beautiful form that is sushumna – rising three and a half feet from the crown of the head and extending over the top of the head. And its function? It is a probe, specifically designed to pick up and express the everything, HAM. From the crown of the head to the base of the spine, those three and a half feet, are an instrument designed to vibrate and express the appearance of creation. Exactly in the center is the three-sided structure, whose entire function is to radiate and vibrate the presence of the guru. I think it's very instructive and very important to note that this triangular structure is inside the contours of the body. It's not even just an eighth of an inch above the crown of the head – it's at the very crown. It's at the point where the sushumna changes its dedication; there's a little skip.

During shaktipat, the guru's role is to switch that little formation on. In most people it's not switched on yet. So, as a guru giving shaktipat, you just go around and hit the ON switch. Simple. Then that profound energy that is the guru, that is all-pervasive and present at the creation, duration and dissolution of existence, both for the individual and for the creation itself, begins to operate. This then produces the interpretation of the everything to the nothing.

In spiritual theory, everything is backwards. The true everything can never be seen, has never been seen. The true nothing, the creation, you see everywhere. This idea of reverse is really true. Everything is opposite of what it appears. You see this idea everywhere.

If we were to look for an analog or simile to what this triangular shape is, we could easily think of it as a radar array. It is designed to capture the vibration of the Guru Shakti and conduct it into the system – that very high and very pure light that operates on both sides of the spectrum. The guru operates inside the appearance of the creation; the guru also operates in the absolute emptiness of the ocean. All that force, *all of that force*, which is infinite, beyond infinite, beyond infinite...is here. It comes through the guru array, the three-sided shape at the crown of the head. It's here.

Why is it here? Because it's everywhere. If it's truly everywhere, you can't be excluded, because you are a part of everywhere. What's missing is you just simply don't quite understand how you're put together, and what is really going on with the design of your human form. You've been caught in the thrall of the mind, the incredible phantasmagoria of the relationship of the mind and the senses. Because the senses are hard-wired in to the brain, they've produced a kind of empiricism that has blotted out a subtler and far more important understanding of your essential nature.

This in turn has led to a snowballing effect of what we call cause-and-effect, karma. Action founded in false understanding is a cause, which must produce an effect; and thus karma is generated. Because it is based on an untruth, it is a false refuge. It exists by virtue of an accumulative, snowballing chain of cause and effect. But compare that phenomena to the recognition of a genuine truth, such as the nature of the guru and the fact that what is here is everywhere and what is everywhere is here. These point to a genuine truth. A single instant of recognition of that truth can wipe away oceans of false understanding in an instant. Why? Because it's true; that's the power of truth.

This is why when we generate the guru yoga we draw the presence of the guru to the crown of the head. Why? Because that's where the seat of the guru is already; it's not a matter of imagination. We're just using the power of our attention to assemble a reality that is already present. Then we use it as a doorway into a very deep, mysterious and profound matter.

This idea that what is here is everywhere, and what is everywhere is here... Even the absence of existence is here; even emptiness is here; even the void is here. From the standpoint of what is here is everywhere, the void is as much a reality as any other. Why? It can be conceived of in imputed terms. When you gain access to the void, it becomes an incredible instrument to draw your attention into that inconceivable quality that we call emptiness. It's a hard thing to conceive of, isn't it? Emptiness. To even conceive of it is to skip off the surface of it. But in the spirit of the day, the spirit of the universal teacher, I'm pointing out something essentially true. We're celebrating the spirit of the guru. It is a day for truth.

The guru itself, is everywhere. It's a universal, eternal spirit, that is here. If you understand this about yourself, it will change your life forever. It bypasses all of those ideas of confusion, forgetfulness, fear – oh, everybody's favorite: unworthiness. You're already worthy. Simply realize and recognize the truth that everything is here, the guru is here.

I want to stay on this idea of form is function. It's

important to understand how you're put together, and not hold to an imagined version of something. If you take a watch apart, and you put it back together how you imagined it should go, it's probably not going to work. You put it back together exactly how it's supposed to be put together, and it works perfectly. That's exactly like how you are. There's a way you operate.

This idea of the connection to the guru leads to everything. It is the source of endless light, and it's designed to do one thing: to illuminate you, to awaken you. You need only accept it on its own terms, and everything will follow. It can't not.

As we begin our Guru Purnima celebration, we plug in to the great ocean of the guru and draw it to the deepest space within. We employ the basic principles that are intrinsic to the human structure; the very operation of the sushumna, conducting the vibration of everything and nothing, which spontaneously arises within each cycle of the breath as the SoHam.

Relaxing deeply into each cycle, the ascending and descending force, the SO and HAM, and the space between the breaths, we let go of our attachment to the physical body, we let go of our attachment to the subtle physical body, we let go of our attachment to the body of mental formation, and plunge straight into the fourth body, the fourth state that lies at the center of being, striking it like lightning or a thunderbolt with every breath. Let's begin our Guru Purnima by plunging into the ocean of the guru nature, the guru shakti, through the gateway of the guru. (meditation)

We have opened our Guru Purnima intensive with the profound idea that everything is here; that the skill and capability of learning to harvest the spontaneously arising force of life within yourself leads to everything. If you can understand this idea, in an instant your sadhana will go to light speed. Once it has been kindled by the touch of the guru, the effectiveness of the inner meshing of consciousness and the presence of the guru's grace, awakens, activates, illuminates, realizes and recognizes everything within oneself as oneself, as God.

Our opening session is an explanation of this profound idea, and the meditation is a demonstration that the guru arises within you as you. Everything that is here is everywhere. To imply otherwise would be to state that there is a second reality. This is what the yoga tantra is about − specifically the ability to harvest the indwelling energies, and express them in their totality, within you as you.

The human form is an incomparable instrument. Once you understand it and know how to make it work, you already have everything you need. It's a powerful idea, even if a somewhat disturbing idea. It puts everything at hand. But this is the secret; it's why it works.

So we come to see that the guru dwells within you as you. We see that the very intention of God and the very intention of the guru are one and the same thing, and manifest within you as your own higher nature. Not only that, but that you also have an instrument that is designed to pick up the vibration of the Guru.

The organ of the eye is present so that the sense of sight can be experienced in the field of sight. The organ of the ear is present so that sound can be heard in the field of sound. In the same way, the seat of the guru, which is present within you at the crown of the head, is an instrument, an organ if you will, that is designed to do one thing: focus the vibration of the guru within you as you. Inasmuch as form is function, even in its dormant condition, it operates as a gateway to higher thought, to intuitive thought, and so provides the opportunity to pick your way through the dangers, obstacles and terrors of this universe, and come through to a point where you are capable of experiencing joy.

The idea of inherent joy is profound. One can easily and safely say that it is joy that everyone and everything seeks in their existence – without exception, period. Joy arises inside the template of countless sentient beings and takes countless formations, but always being only one thing: joy. It is the desire for that, which is behind every action. As we become more cultivated and more evolved, we see our concept of what joy is changes. Joy is the fulfillment and the manifestation of love. Intrinsic in the desire for joy and the desire for love, we have a developing ability, or capability, that we sometimes call skillful means.

At the seat of everyone's actions, we see the desire for joy. Nobody deliberately sets out and generates any form of action to guarantee their own misery. What we see at the heart or the seed of every single action and every single desire, is the expression of joy and the desire to express that joy and to experience that joy. Yet how many times even with the purest intention of heart, the purest intention of desire – does our action lead us to misery, pain and suffering? This is often the basis of art and literature. One of the most famous stories of all time, Romeo and Juliet, is the tale of how the purest form of love imaginable brings about the most epic pain and suffering. You see in that story how very complex realities can emerge out of the desire and karma of self-arising desire, out of desirelessness, and out of the force of the desire of others.

This is the way karma is. It is that volume of karma that distorts the purest of desires, and that comes between the desire of love and joy with great intensity. Why? Because they arise simultaneously – they're not two things. The love and the joy that is the seat of every action is also the karma of previous actions born of desire, the karma of actions generated without the slightest desire, and most interestingly, also the karma of the desire of others that are attached to you. Just the desire for love and joy is not a guarantee for the fulfillment of that love or that joy.

So we begin to see that there is an unseen factor that is highly determinative in the resolution of joy. It doesn't just happen. Like everything else, there's a trick to it – and this is the quality of skill. The formal term is skillful means. The ability to generate intention and fully bring about its resolution takes the highest form of intention. It also takes the highest form of love, because it must generate the completion and the fulfillment of love, the completion and fulfillment of joy.

You must be present on both sides of the coin. You

must be present in the light and you also must be present in the darkness. It is out of the shadows that the obstacles emerge; those things that we don't wish to know about, don't wish to feel. Why? Because to touch them is to experience pain. It is a trick of consciousness that uses the subconscious psyche and the unconscious psyche, whereby we objectify and make 'other' those forces that come out of the shadows. Carl Jung very beautifully and perfectly entitled the shadow "the other".

Though in reality it is not the other – it is ourselves. You have to understand that. There's not a second thing; there's not one thing and a second thing. Everything arises simultaneously. You have to get used to that. The highest ideal, the highest cause, the greatest love, the truest desire, the truest joy has its obstacle by its very nature. The very opposite side of your own nature can confound.

As you get to know a person, more often than not you see that they are their own greatest enemy. They can't bring to equilibrium the two sides of their nature. They'll tend to be all one or all the other, or more one than the other. If they're too much just in the light, they're not realistic about the shadows in the world; if they're too much of the darkness, they turn self-destructive. So you have to illuminate both sides.

In my experience, I've come to see that love is the ability to navigate the way. Love is the only thing that will give you the attention to stay on line and skillfully navigate the shoals that you must get through to complete your gesture. If you soar high in the air and charge off blindly, you will quickly come to grief. You have to stay open and alert at each step, because every situation is in constant flux. So you have to learn to draw on that power of love, like an unspooling thread that never breaks. You must come to know your own shadow nature and face the obstacles brought about by your own desire-based activity, and by the desires of others, which is as powerful a karma as your own.

Every interaction is so complicated. In a single conversation, you think and say one thing, and the person listens to you, and they think and say something else. Both are producing the event. You escalate that equation: you hit somebody with a rock, hey – they want to hit you with a rock. If you run away fast enough so they don't have time to hit you with a rock, they still want to hit you with a rock. The intention of that person will follow you through lifetime after lifetime – it'll stick to you. That's an example of what I mean when I say 'the karma of others'... and it will find a way to resolve itself.

I like the idea of life as a journey; the facing of obstacles, difficulties, enemies, conflicts, and bringing about successful resolution by navigating and getting through. We start to see that at one level of attention it's by hook or by crook: what I want is more important than anything else. And perhaps you're strong enough to get so far down the road; you're stronger than this person and that person. But there's always somebody stronger somewhere down the road, and you meet defeat; that teaches you a lesson.

The way you face obstacles is one of the highest forms of skill. In any situation that you are in, break down the components of it – there are psychological and emotional aspects, there's the application of action, there is the intent, will, desire and ideal. These are the components of every situation. When you're in a situation or you come into conflict with someone; try to recognize the ideal of your source of conflict: what is their ideal, what do they want, what is their joy? Then read their intent – what is their intention flowing off of that desire, flowing off of that joy. What did they mean to do? What did they desire to do? And then, finally, what is their application, what is their action, what is their kriya and what are they doing about it? You need to know all these things to skillfully read every situation. If you leave any part of it out, you're going to be misinforming yourself, and most likely leaving yourself open to making a mistake. That mistake will blossom into a force that will hook you in some way, and cause your goal to be turned, stalled or defeated.

In Tai Chi, there's a principle called neutrality. In any given conflict there are a thousand ratios or relationships – and no one relationship in those thousand relationships is worth making a life-and-death stand over. You're standing in this space and a person comes toward you. "Oh, you want to occupy this space?" Rather than meet their force with your own force, you simply step out of the way and give them that space. All that energy is saved. More often than not, they'll just blow right past you.

Now they're behind you and you can keep going. No one position is absolute. You need to take a subtle reading of these various ratios in the situation. In other words, what is their will, what is their ideal, what is their cause, what is their action? They will always be present. The trick is not to make it personal. It's karma playing out.

What you want is the fulfillment and completion of the ideal of love, the completion of the ideal of joy. This formula starts out small: you're a ten-year old kid, and you want a candy bar. You get your candy bar; you're in the third grade, and the kid in the fourth grade beats you up and takes it from you – you lost your candy bar. But things become more and more sophisticated as we move up, and as we move into more serious gambits, more serious plays of life. The equation doesn't change that much, the stakes just go up. We begin to see that there are stages of love, stages of joy and stages of completion.

In spiritual life, we're not after a philosophical victory. We want the completion of the path, the completion and fulfillment of the awakening process. We're not after a theoretical or Pyrrhic victory, but genuine awakening. On the spiritual path, the stakes are never higher – the highest stakes are your life and the terms of your life.

You'll find that the greater and greater the awakening, the greater and greater the light that will flow in the system. The more light in the system, the more spiritual power you have access to. The more spiritual power you have access to, the higher rate of performance the matrix of your mind-body-being will be capable of. The higher rate of performance your mind-body-being matrix is capable of, the more subtle and refined the application of your skill set of arousal of desire, the application of your will, which is your intent, and the application of your desire and will to your actions will be. If your love is strong, it will stay like a searchlight on the path, constantly illuminating every step. You'll be able to adjust yourself as needed, step by step.

What is it that is usually the cause of defeat or making a serious mistake? Mistakes are only classified as those things that cost. If you make a mistake, it costs you two things: it costs you energy and it costs you time. That's how you can tell. It's fatigue – you just get tired; you run out of energy, you can't think straight, you burn out, you start making mistakes, and all of a sudden, you've gone as far as you're going; your ship seems to just stall out, bank over to the side, get stuck in the reeds – you kind of float there and get a sunburn. "Why isn't my boat moving?"

In my experience, I've seen that there's a direct relationship between love and ability. We express skill and ability in what we love. We call forth that love and bring it up and out; we apply that love to what we care about, so much so that one could say that love is ability. It's the question that every teacher has for every student: What is it that you care about? What do you love? Your behavior reflects it. To what extent does your intent align with your action? It's very revealing. If you think you love one thing, but your actions say another, then you need to cultivate a greater alignment between your own intention and your own action. Almost everyone will gain from that.

One of the things you'll see when you run into the masters is that their ideal, their intention and their action are a singularity – there's not the slightest gap. That's the force. That's spiritual power. You can always find a parking place. This is the same idea that we're talking about today.

What is here is everywhere. It doesn't go anywhere. It all occurs: it arises and resolves, as a disequilibrium that seeks equilibrium. If you come to know yourself, you can feel where the disequilibrium is. Just consult your own nature. Yes, it's oftentimes most difficult to see yourself – but you also have to get over that. In spiritual life, you spend a lot of time meditating. What are you doing while you're meditating? You're seeing everything, and it is both light and shadow. Truly speaking, oftentimes what's most interesting about a person, is what is going on in their shadow nature. That's where the energy is coming from. It has to become illuminated and it has to get directed, or it'll produce conflict and destruction.

We were talking about this at the summer retreat:

part of the spiritual path is opening up the cellar door and going down the steps. What's down there? It's not walled off. It has to be known. Everybody has a healthy fear of what's in the darkness, partly because there's a lot of potency there.

It's always best to have alliance before you face unknown difficulties. This is where the guru comes in; this is where shaktipat comes in, providing a quality of illumination and equilibrium, and acting as a kind of tether. As I was explaining this morning, the seat of the guru is inside your own mind, it's inside your own body, present as your own higher nature, which is a composite compound of body, speech and mind.

This is what the Bodhicitta is all about – it is the concept that enlightenment is spontaneously present. The intent and the action need to come more thoroughly and more constantly in contact with that ideal. As we build spiritual force, we are more capable of illuminating and displacing greater amounts of darkness. This creates the equilibrium between desire – which is born of joy, love and intention – and action, which is the effective application. And it is most certainly trial and error.

What is here is everywhere, and everything is here.

The ideal of enlightenment is present; the intention of the path is present. In between the ideal, intent and the application of action, we have all of the karma, the cause-and-effect residue of desire-based actions of previous lifetimes. Those actions which are without desire, and those actions and karmas that are born of the desire of others. Every time you have a thought of a person, you generate a relationship that's a cause; and the energy of that produces an effect, and that produces a karma. Shankaracharya spoke of the mind as a mirror, and taught that you have to clear the mirror every day and make it spotless. But in ten seconds it's covered with dust again. The dust is all of the karmic seeds that are ripening every second, ripening every second, ripening every second.

This is why I give you that picture of love as the ability to stay constantly present through every situation. It's a burning light and allows you to see what's really happening. You're not telling a story that's a cover for another story; you're just seeing it directly, experiencing it directly, seeing the thing in itself. You can then look in between this relationship – between ideal, desire, the expression of will as intent and the application of skillful means as action.

One of the guidelines of all action is a quality called detachment. Don't be attached to the fruits of the action. Give rise to action and skill, with the full force of your spirit; but allow the fruit of that action to be what it is. Offer it to God. Don't try to possess it. If you try to possess it, you end up owning it and it becomes your karma; it attaches to you. If you stay unattached to the fruit of action, if you offer it to God, then it just floats out into the ocean and it becomes like adding your light to the sum of light. Again, it's a good rule of thumb. Everybody that gets good at the path, gets good at doing that.

I think we can draw a straight line between this idea of non-attachment to the Tai Chi concept of neutrality. "Oh, you want this space? You can have it". Instead of having to make a big to-do out of it, simply step six inches to the left; they've got that space, and they're still going in that direction. The whole thing is done so that you can go merrily on your way. Compare the amount of energy it took you to move six inches out of the way, compared to some life-and-death struggle over... what? It's a picture of non-attachment versus attachment. Let things come, let things go; let people come, let people go; let situations come, let situations go. It's constantly unfolding karma. It will happen anyway.

Another way to say it is that skillful means is learning how to pick and choose your fights. Fight the fights that really count; don't allow yourself to be distracted and bled off into the countless skirmishes that lead to nothing.

What's most important is to keep your eye on the ball; keep your eye on the prize, the true source of love, the true source of joy. It does not arise from outside of you, it arises within you, as you.

In our great lunar celebration of the guru, we are expressing the deep, profound and mysterious nature of the guru, which is present within us. As we sit throughout the day, we feel the power of the guru unfold within us, as us. Essentially speaking, all the systems of consciousness are switched on. The guru's nature is one of awakening. Imagine if every single system of awareness within yourself was on and active, operating at optimum efficiency. It is incredible spiritual force and the power of irresistible transformation and change.

Today we opened the gateway of the guru, and allowed that force to flow into the vase of our human forms, flooding the four bodies and all of the subtle systems of consciousness.

Very Good.

Good Night.

GLOSSARY

Ashrama ~ Refers to the Vedic view that there are four stages of life – the stage of study and self-discipline; the stage of householder and person of the world; the stage of contemplation and gradual withdrawal from worldly connections; and the stage of total renunciation.

Atman ~ (from the Sanskrit root at = "to breathe") The transcendental Self or Spirit. It is the eternal, superconscious, Supreme Soul, and Divine Self within each individual. The spiritual essence of all individual human beings.

Bardo ~ In Tibetan, this literally means "the interval". There are usually six bardos that are spoken of. In this book, Mark is referring to the bardo thodol, the intermediate state that enlightens upon contact. (see "The Bardo Thodol" by Mark Griffin). The six bardos are: the bardo of the waking state (the interval between birth and death); the bardo of the dream state (the interval between going to sleep at night and awakening in the morning); the bardo of meditation (the interval between the breaths); the bardo of death, chikhai bardo (the interval between life and the afterlife); the bardo of luminosity, the chonyid bardo (the interval between death and rebirth); and the bardo of rebirth, the sidpabardo (the interval between the afterlife and the new experience of the waking state). The bardo thodol comprises the three last bardos, chikhai, chonyid and sidpa, as it is possible to spontaneously gain enlightenment during any of these states by direct recognition of reality.

Bodhicitta ~ ("the essence of enlightenment") Formed by the heart/mind connection, it represents the union of formation and emptiness. Bodhicitta reflects the truth of enlightenment, which does not come from an outside agency, but comes from within you as you. Alignment with the Bodhicitta produces an irresistible force for awakening.

Brahmarandra ~ ("the hole of Brahman") Located in the thousand-petaled chakra at the crown of the head, it is the soft spot at the brain found in infants; the point where the infusion of life takes place in the human being. It is just underneath the skull embedded in the upper layer of the cerebrum, which is the part of the brain that is dedicated to the highest brain functions. This is also the seat of the Guru. It is the superior place to exit the body upon death. (See the concept of "phowa" in The Bardo Thodol by Mark Griffin).

Chakras ~ (Sanskrit for "circle" or "wheel") There are seven main chakras or energy centers located in the subtle body. These nerve plexes are located along the center of the body in the sushumna, the subtle central channel where the nadis converge. The chakras begin at the base of the spine where the Kundalini lies coiled. The base chakra with four petals is called Muladhara. The 2nd chakra, Svadhisthana, has six petals and is located at the base of the reproductive organs. The 3rd chakra, Manipura, has 10 petals and is located in the naval region. The 4th chakra, Anahata, with its sixteen petals, is located in the heart region. The 5th chakra, Vishuddhi, has sixteen petals and is located at the base of the throat. The 6th chakra, Ajna, has two petals and is found between the eyebrows, at the third eye. The 7th chakra is the Sahasrar, found at the crown of the head with its 1000 petals.

Chit ~ (from the Sanskrit root cit = "to think, to be aware, to perceive") Awareness, consciousness, knowledge; the unseen power of consciousness. To the awakened being, chit appears as scintillating blue particles of light.

Dharma ~ (from the Sanskrit root dhr = "to uphold, to sustain, to carry") That which supports or sustains the universe. The ultimate law; the essential duty; the righteous way. To say that one performs one's dharma means that one is acting from total alignment with one's own life's highest purpose. It is the basic principle of divine law and the basis of all social and moral order.

Dhyana ~ (from the Sanskrit root "dhi" = intellect) An advanced state of meditation beyond *dharana* where the mind is engaged in concentration or single-pointed focus. *Dhyana* is the stage of meditation in which the mind is able to comprehend its oneness with everything, and all mental activity ceases, so that all sense of separate Self disappears.

Emptiness ~ A state which is beyond all imputed terms (see imputed terms below). It has nothing to do with an empty or lonely feeling or an empty glass of water. It is the state of void, containing nothing and yet containing everything. There is nothing similar to it and nothing different from it.

Fire Mountain Retreat ~ The Hard Light Center of Awakening retreat center located in Nimboli, Ganeshpuri, India, about 80 kms. north of Mumbai in the Thane district. Located in front of the majestic mountain of Mandagni. www.firemountainretreat.org

Four Bodies ~ Physical, subtle physical, causal and supra causal. The physical body is the body that we relate to and feel is the real body. The subtle physical body is the energetic body, also referred to as the astral body. The causal body is the body without physical form. It is mind itself and encompasses the mental faculties of manas (mind), buddhi (intellect), ahamkara (ego), and infinitely more levels that become revealed upon awakening. The supra causal body is the fourth body and is the Atman, oneness with consciousness itself.

Ganeshpuri ~ (See Fire Mountain Retreat) The site where Baba Muktananda has his mahasamadhi tomb, as well as the site of his Guru Bhagawan Nityananda's Temple and mahasamadhi shrine. This was a small rural jungle village until Bhagawan Nityananda came and settled there, making it his home. It is a site of many spontaneously arisen Shiva lingams, as well as seats of Shakti, and is a very important spiritual location, sacred to the Siddhas.

Gordian Knot ~ A well known legend associated with Alexander the Great, which held that whoever could unbind the knot would become the next king of Asia. Many people came and tried to untie the knot, without success. When Alexander was unable to untie the knot, he quickly sliced through it with his sword. The Gordian Knot is now used as a metaphor for solving any difficult problem by using a bold stroke, instead of by using conventional means.

Gunas ~ ("strand, thread or quality") The three basic qualities or attributes of nature which underlie all manifestation: sattva, rajas and tamas. All manifest creation is made up of a combination of these three gunas. Sattva is ruled by Vishnu, is of the nature of integration, and is characterized as white. It is the highest frequency and is buoyant with light. Sattva is knowledge, happiness, integration and infinite existence without differentiation. Rajas is ruled by Brahma and characterized as red. The nature of rajas is cyclic revolution – passion, churning and violent spinning – that which is spinning towards the center and that which is spinning out into infinite expansion. Tamas is ruled by Shiva. It is characterized as the abysmal, infinite black. It is a quality that is so dense that it is thought of as a black hole. Nothing emerges from it. It is absolute, dense, infinite blackness, with no light emerging and all qualities crushed into a compression so deep that nothing can be discerned. It is the origin of creation. To say that the Guru is beyond the three gunas means that he is the source of creation even before creation itself came into manifestation.

Guru Purnima ~ Celebrated in India as a major holiday on the full moon during the month of Ashada (July-August), Guru Purnima is one of the most auspicious days for offering prayers to the Guru.

Guru Shakti ~ The power of the Guru. The Guru principle. (see Shakti)

Ida ~ Known as the moon nadi, this channel or prana current ascends up the left side of the central channel, the sushumna. It is connected to the parasympathetic nervous system and has a calming and cooling effect on the mind when it is activated. It originates at the base of the spine and terminates at the left nostril. The ida is essentially empty in nature and is of the reflective quality of mind. (See nadis, sushumna and pingala)

Imputed Terms ~ To attribute a quality to something. The ocean of consciousness that is referred to in the Guru Gita is beyond all qualities. Notice that even when you call something holy or sacred, it sets up a relationship with other things. If something is holy, there must be something that is more holy or less holy, and on and on it goes. To say something is beyond imputed terms is to understand that there is nothing to compare it to, nothing to match it up against. It also means that it is the same for everyone who experiences it. Normally when we experience something, we each have a unique perception of it. For example, smelling a rose brings up different impressions for each person and an entirely different impression for a honeybee. This is not the case with that which is beyond imputed terms. Thus, that which is beyond imputed terms is referred to as empty, devoid of all relative qualities.

Ishvara ~ (from the Sanskrit root ish = "to rule") The Supreme Lord. The Eternal One. All that humanity can know of God, both transcendent and immanent. The fourth tattva, supreme divinity. (see tattva)

Janglidas Maharaj ~ Known as "Om Gurudev" to his devotees, Janglidas is a realized great being. Janglidas' message is that God lives in our heart and is attained through meditation. He founded the Ashram of Nerla in the Sangli district. He is also noted for having done his early sadhana in Yeola with Baba Muktananda. He honored Hard Light by traveling to Fire Mountain Retreat in 2008 for its inauguration.

Japa / Ajapa (see SoHam)

Kali ~ The consort of the Lord Shiva. The dark form of the Goddess associated with destruction and rebirth. Also known as the Goddess Durga. Usually represented as a black naked woman with a demonic face wearing a necklace of skulls, dripping blood.

Karma ~ ("action") The universal law of cause and effect governing the cycle of birth, death and rebirth. The concept that the accumulated effect of every action performed, whether good or bad, comes back to impact a person's destiny, lifetime after lifetime.

Kriya ~ Physical action. Gross physical movements or more subtle emotional and mental movements that are initiated by the awakened Kundalini to purify the body. These movements give the seeker the necessary endurance and strength required to deal with the higher energy states of awakened consciousness.

Kundalini ~ ("coiled one") The primordial Shakti which lies dormant, coiled like a serpent, three and a half times at the base of the spine in the muladhara chakra. Once this mystical energy or life force is awakened, it then ignites the quest for spiritual knowledge in the seeker. Through shaktipat, a Siddha master is able to activate this divine cosmic energy so that it can arise and expand consciousness through the purification that it brings about.

Last Chopper Out Of Saigon ~ This refers to Operation "Frequent Wind", the emergency evacuation of almost all of the American civilian and military personnel, along with tens of thousands of South Vietnamese civilians in Saigon at the end of the Vietnam War in April,1975. This was the largest helicopter evacuation in history. As Mark describes: "There is a famous moment at the capitulation of the war. At the top of the embassy in Saigon there is this building, and atop that is a turret, and then another turret. And everybody was making their escape out of the city. The Viet Cong and the Khmer Rouge were coming in, and there was one last chopper coming in. Everybody was climbing on the building, and climbing up the sides of the building, trying to get onto that chopper. It was the last chopper out of Saigon. It's a famous moment and it repeats itself in history."

Mahamudra ~ (from the Sanskrit root: maha = "great"; mud = "joy"; ra = "to give") Great seal or great symbol. At the most esoteric level, this is the seal between the infinite ocean of consciousness and the manifest world of creation. Mudras are gestures or expressions.

For instance, the thumb and forefinger held together is known in yoga as one of the more well-known hand mudras. Many of the statues of deities are shown with the hands and body in various mudra positions. They also act as energetic seals of authority.

Mandala ~ ("circle" or "center") Symbolizes the wholeness of creation.

Mano-nash ~ The dissolution of the mind. The term nasha means 'destruction'. It is not the willful obliteration of one's rational faculties. Rather it stands for the yogic process of transcending the conventional mind, which revolves around the pivot of the ego-identity.

Marpa ~ Marpa Lotsawa was the founder of the Kagyupa order of Vajrayana Buddhism, a tradition of Tibetan Buddhism. He lived from 1012 - 1096 CE. He was the disciple of Naropa and the guru of Milarepa. He was also a renowned translator and a tantric master.

Medicine Wheel ~ Represents Native American spirituality. The Medicine Wheel symbolizes the individual journey we must each take to find our own way. Most wheels have a basic pattern with a center of stones and an outer ring of stones that form spokes radiating from the center. The Medicine Wheel contains the four cardinal directions and the four sacred colors. The center of the circle represents the eternal fire and the rest of the circle represents the circle of life.

MentalPhysics of Joshua Tree ~ "A Sacred Space in the High Desert". Founded by Edwin J. Dingle in 1941 as a place of meditation and healing. Located 35 minutes from Palm Springs, Joshua Tree Retreat has beautiful vistas of the desert, mountains, and centuries of Joshua Trees. Used as a retreat site by Hard Light Center of Awakening. www.mentalphysics.net

Milarepa ~ Jetsun Milarepa was the foremost disciple of Marpa Lotsawa and lived in Tibet approximately 1040 - 1123 CE. He is considered to be one of Tibet's most well renowned folk heroes, as well as an enlightened poet and yogi. He is famous for his songs of spiritual realization and his devotion to his guru Marpa.

Mount Meru ~ In Hindu mythology, this sacred mountain is thought to be the center of all spiritual universes. Many of the Hindu temples in India have been built as representations of Mount Meru. During retreats, Mark Griffin creates a symbolic Mount Meru by building a mound of rice in the center of the back puja.

With its base rooted in hell and its peak in the heavens, Mount Meru represents the center of the universe. It sits surrounded by seven rings of mountains each separated from the other by seven oceans. At its summit is a golden palace where the Hindu god Indra lives.

Nadis ~ A very complex psychic network of 72,000 subtle fibers, interconnecting the chakras in the subtle body. The life force, the prana, circulates through the nadis. The sushumna, ida and pingala are the three principle nadis. (See sushumna, ida, pingala)

Nimboli ~ A small village just outside of Ganeshpuri, that is home to the Fire Mountain Retreat. (See "Fire Mountatin Retreat" or "Ganeshpuri")

Nirvikalpa (see Samadhi)

Om Point ~ Absolute ground zero for reality at a universal level, which pervades the totality of everything.

Pashyanti ~ ("that which can be seen or visualized") The second level of sound; the finest impulse of speech. Pashyanti represents the intellectual consciousness, where speech is intuitively connected to the object. Its seat is in the navel or the manipura chakra. The four levels of speech, from most-refined to most-concrete, are

Para, Pashyanti, Madhyama and Vaikhari. They correspond to the four states of consciousness.

Pingala ~ Known as the sun nadi, this channel or prana current ascends up the right side of the central channel, the sushumna. It is connected to the sympathetic nervous system and has a heated or energizing effect on the mind when it is activated. It originates near the base of the spine, between the first and second chakras, and terminates at the right nostril. Almost the entire malini, the alphabet of the creation, is suspended inside the pingala. It is the expression of the creation of the world. (See nadis, sushumna and ida)

Prana ~ The vital life force energy that sustains the body. It animates all physical and material forms including the human body and is absorbed into the body through the breath. There are five principal forms of prana: the rising force known as prana; the descending force known as apana; the cyclical revolution force known as samana; the splitting and attracting force known as vayana; and the force of infusion known as udana.

Puja ~ (from the Sanskrit root: puj = "to honor, to venerate, to serve") To worship; actions performed in worship to show respect to a deity or high being. Puja can also refer to an altar that has images or statues of a Guru or high deities, along with sacred objects and flowers used for worship.

Pyrrhic Victory ~ a victory with devastating cost to the victor. The phrase is named after King Pyrrhus of Epirus, whose army suffered irreplaceable casualties in defeating the Romans at Heraclea in 280 BC and Asculum in 279 BC during the Pyrrhic War.

Rasa ~ (from the Sanskrit root: ras = "to be conscious of a sensation") The essence, flavor or nectar of a thing.

REM ~ Rapid Eye Movement. The 5th phase of sleep where dreams and vivid hallucinatory imaging occur and the eyes move quickly back and forth.

Sadhana ~ (from the Sanskrit root saadh = "to go straight to the goal") Spiritual practices or disciplines designed to lead to enlightenment.

Samadhi ~ (from the Sanskrit root sam = "completely together"; and dhaa = "to hold") To hold completely together, as in one-pointed concentration or absorption. The eighth and final limb of yoga as expounded by the great sage Patanjali. The union of oneness and the highest state of super-consciousness, which occurs through the full awakening and unfoldment of the kundalini shakti. There are four states of samadhi: laya samadhi, savikalpa samadhi, nirvikalpa samadhi and sahaj samadhi.

Samsara ~ ("continual movement") The cyclic existence of reincarnation: birth, death and rebirth or transmigration. This word points to the idea of being stuck in the relative ever-changing aspect of creation without experience of the absolute non-changing reality. The conditioned endless karmic cycle of worldly existence that is transcended once one achieves the highest state of enlightenment.

Samskara ~ Mental or subconscious impressions stored in the sushumna from this life or past lives that influence us by forming patterns and tendencies that form the basis of our beliefs and our personalities and thus guide our decisions and actions. To those capable of seeing the subtle body, the samskaras which reside in the sushumna and along the nadis of the subtle body, are said to appear like small kernels of rice, colored from white to grey to black. The black samskaras are impressions from negative events, while the white are from more positive events. In either case, all samskaras are an obstacle to storing enough spiritual power to gain full realization.

Sankalpa ~ (from the Sanskrit root: sam = "completely"; klrp = "to come into existence") Spiritual resolve, volition, intention, determination, thought, will, mental activity, directed towards a specific result.

Shakti ~ ("energy" or "power") Often referred to as the Goddess Shakti, the consort of Shiva. It is the life giving force, the potency of the female energy, the creative principle and its expression. Through training with a true Guru, one's spiritual energy or shakti builds up or accumulates, gradually empowering the seeker with the ability to realize the truth.

Shaktipat ~ (shakti = "energy" and pat = "descent or falling down") The transmission or descent of grace from a Guru to his disciple through touch, sight, sacred word or thought. Shaktipat activates the dormant kundalini in a person who is open to receiving it. This transference of energy from the Guru to the disciple is known as the bestowal of grace. Shaktipat is a gift given by the Guru.

Shankaracharya ~ (Acharya = "teacher, guide, instructor") Shankara was an 8th century Hindu scholar and philosopher who died at the age of

33, but during his life, toured India and opened up four learning and education centers in four different parts of India in order to promote Hinduism. These are known as the maths, and are in the north, south, east and west of the country. Shankara was a great non-dualist, who taught that the Infinite Ocean of Consciousness is beyond attributes and all imputed terms. He also expounded on the unity of the individual soul and the universal soul. His teachings consolidated the philosophy of Advaita Vedanta.

Siddha ~ ("one who is accomplished") A perfected being who has realized embodied liberation. One who has attained the state of uninterrupted unity-consciousness and has perfect and permanent identity with the source of all. Baba Muktananda and Bhagawan Nityananda are examples of Siddhas.

SoHam ~ (So = "That"; Ham = "I") A mantra that comes from the natural sound of the inhalation and exhalation of the breath. Thus with each breath the reality is stated "That Am I" – "I am Pure Consciousness". SoHam is equivalent to the mantra Hamsa, "I Am That". The use of the mantra SoHam or Hamsa is known as 'ajapa japa'. Japa means the repetition of a mantra. When 'a' is placed before a Sanskrit word, it creates the opposite meaning. So ajapa means non-repeating. In other words, this is the mantra that is repeated without doing the practice of repetition, because it is naturally being done for us by the breath itself. SO has its root at the first chakra at the base of the spine, while HAM has its root at the crown of the head at the sahasrar. SO represents all of manifest creation, while HAM represents the ocean of pure consciousness.

Sushumna ~ The central prana channel through which the Kundalini rises. Starting at the base of the spine where the Kundalini serpent power is coiled, the sushumna rises up through the center of the body to the crown of the head. This subtle principle nerve is the only nadi that connects the first six chakras with the seventh chakra at the crown of the head. It, along with the ida and pingala nadis, are the three principle nadis of the subtle human body. (See nadis, ida and pingala)

Tantra / Tantrica ~ (a loom; weaving or continuity) Sacred texts, one of several esoteric traditions rooted in Hinduism, that are studied in order to expand consciousness.

Tiger's Milk ~ Absolute, penetrating pure energy. Mark Griffin says "It is said to be so pure that a single drop is enough to shatter the container that holds it, if that container is not pure. Baba

Muktananda was fond of saying that a vessel had to be pure gold to hold a drop of Tiger's Milk.

Tree of Life ~ An ancient mystical concept used in cultures throughout the world symbolic of knowledge, ascension, the cycle of life and eternity. With its branches reaching up and its roots reaching down, the tree of life symbolizes the link between the three worlds: heaven, earth and the underworld. It is that which unites them all. It is also often shown as an inverted tree superimposed on the figure of the human body, with its root system in the sahasrar and the space over the crown of the head, and the branches spreading throughout the nadis of the subtle body of the human form.

Vajra ~ ("thunder" or "diamond") Thought of as a thunderbolt, the weapon of Indra represents adamantine strength. In Tibetan and Buddhist culture the vajra, the "diamond" scepter, is used by deities as a ritual tool and represents the Bodhicitta, the mind of enlightenment. (see Bodhicitta)

Vase Meditation ~ A specific kind of meditation taught by Mark Griffin that is a combination of Hindu and Tibetan ideologies. The human form is like a vase that is open at the top and contained on all sides. The impulse of prana descends to fill the human form like a vase filled with water. Vase meditation also has the goal of gathering and storing energy and power, specifically the bodhicitta.

Vortex (Power) ~ A spinning, powerful, often turbulent, flow of energy that involves constant intense action around a center. Like a whirlwind or tornado. During the 2008 Hard Light retreat in Varanasi, India, Mark Griffin said: "When I look out over the city of Varanasi, I see thousands of vortices. Most of them look like tornados. They're like swirling energy fields that start wide and go down to a point and touch the Earth. Descending from the atmosphere, they go up about a thousand feet, like a giant dome. That's the true city. It is mind blowing. I've never seen anything like it anywhere else. Usually places of power are in desolate areas. The fact that there is a human city present here is very unique."

Vyasa ~ ("compiler" or "arranger") One of the best known figures of Hinduism, Vyasa was the author of the Hindu epic, The Mahabharata, as well as the Puranas. He compiled the Vedas into four parts and was thereafter referred to as Veda Vyasa.

The all day Intensive "What Is Here Is Everywhere", featured in the last chapter of this book, held some particularly profound meditation sessions. These have been compiled into an 80 minute guided meditation, interspersed with music for meditation.

If you would like to deepen your study of this subject, visit the Hard Light Online Store (www.hardlight.org/store/) where you'll find this meditation now available as a CD or as a digital download.

Other Books by Mark Griffin

108 Discourses on Awakening

The Bardo Thodol ~ A Golden Opportunity

Samadhi Kunda

Six Session Vajra Guru Yoga

Shri Guru Gita

Kundalini (2009)

Emptiness (2009)

Wheel of Cyclic Existence (2009)

108 Discourses ~ Volume 2 (2009)

~ Jewels ~
Selected Talks from the 2007 & 2008
Weekly Meetings (2009)

These titles and more are available
through our Online Store:
visit www.hardlight.org/store/

Audiobooks by Mark Griffin

Everything and Nothing
India Yatra 2008
Kali and the Guru
Kundalini - 1
Kundalini - 2
Kundalini - 3
Love Is An Act Of Will
MahaShivaratri
Power
Prana Apana
Prana, SoHam, 4 Bodies
Rupa ~ The Blue Pearl
Samadhi Kunda
The Awakener
The Bardo Thodol
The Chöd
The Focal Point Of Intention
The Guru-Disciple Relationship
The Mechanics of Shaktipat
The Perfection of Wisdom
The Recognition of Consciousness
The Six Session Vajra Guru Yoga
The Thread of Continuousness
The Universe
The Wheel of Cyclic Existence
The Grace Waves of Guru Yoga
Varanasi 2008
What Is Here Is Everywhere
What Is Shaktipat?
Zen And The Art Of Cessation, Observation And Samadhi

Guided Meditations by Mark Griffin

Bodhicitta I
Bodhicitta II
Bodhicitta III
Divine Will
Kundalini
Listening To The SoHam
Pranayama
Pratyahara I - Distilled
Pratyahara I - The Five Stages
Pratyahara II
The Awakener
The Breath
The Space Between The Breaths
The Union Of Shiva And Shakti
Tune In To The Guru Radar

These titles and more are available
through our Online Store:
visit www.hardlight.org/store/

Journal ~ Thoughts ~ Notes

Journal ~ Thoughts ~ Notes